Bilingualism Matters

What happens in the brain when learning a second language? Can speaking more than one language provide cognitive benefits over a lifetime? What implications does an increase in bilingualism have for society? And what are the factors that can promote and support bilingualism in children and adults? This book – a translated and adapted version of *Il Cervello Bilingue* (2020) – answers these questions and more, providing the reader with a comprehensive yet concise guide on different topics related to bilingualism. Based on the results of the most recent studies conducted internationally, it discusses recent research findings, explains terminology, and elaborates on the current state of the field, with the aim of providing families and society with suggestions about how to encourage bilingualism. Written in an engaging and accessible style, it takes both academics and readers with no prior knowledge of the field on a journey into the bilingual brain.

Maria Garraffa is Associate Professor in Psycholinguistics at the University of East Anglia and Honorary Fellow of Bilingualism Matters. Her research has contributed to the promotion of language learning across the lifespan.

Antonella Sorace is Professor of Developmental Linguistics at the University of Edinburgh. She is the founding director of the organization Bilingualism Matters, which has branches all over the world.

Maria Vender is Assistant Professor in Educational Linguistics at the University of Verona. Her research interests cover the domains of language acquisition and processing in typical, atypical and bilingual contexts.

Bilingualism Matters
Language Learning Across the Lifespan

Maria Garraffa
University of East Anglia

Antonella Sorace
University of Edinburgh

Maria Vender
University of Verona

Translated and adapted to English by:
John W. Schwieter
Wilfrid Laurier University

Shaftesbury Road, Cambridge CB2 8EA, United Kingdom

One Liberty Plaza, 20th Floor, New York, NY 10006, USA

477 Williamstown Road, Port Melbourne, VIC 3207, Australia

314–321, 3rd Floor, Plot 3, Splendor Forum, Jasola District Centre,
New Delhi – 110025, India

103 Penang Road, #05–06/07, Visioncrest Commercial, Singapore 238467

Cambridge University Press is part of Cambridge University Press & Assessment,
a department of the University of Cambridge.

We share the University's mission to contribute to society through the pursuit of
education, learning and research at the highest international levels of excellence.

www.cambridge.org
Information on this title: www.cambridge.org/9781009333382

DOI: 10.1017/9781009333375

Originally published in Italian as *Il cervello linguistico* by Maria Garraffa, Antonella Sorace
and Maria Vender, © Carocci editore S.p.A, Roma 2020

First published 2023

Printed in the United Kingdom by CPI Group Ltd, Croydon CR0 4YY

A catalogue record for this publication is available from the British Library.

A Cataloging-in-Publication data record for this book is available from the Library of Congress.

ISBN 978-1-009-33338-2 Hardback
ISBN 978-1-009-33336-8 Paperback

....

Maria Garraffa, Antonella Sorace and Maria Vender developed the structure of the book,
selected the materials, and revised the full manuscript in close collaboration. Chapters 1,
3 and 4 are attributed to Maria Garraffa; chapters 2, 5 and 6 to Maria Vender.

CONTENTS

FIGURES

ACKNOWLEDGMENTS

This book would not have been conceived without the constant support of the growing community of international language experts who now have a mission to engage the public with the latest research on bilingualism and language learning and promote bilingualism with any language.

Promoting bilingualism means supporting learning any language at any age: We hope that this book can contribute to reinforcing this view. From a linguistic and cognitive perspective there is no difference between more prestigious and less prestigious languages, and recent research supports the idea that every combination of languages can have positive effects on both the brain and the behavior of bilingual speakers.

We would also like to thank the many organizations, schools, stakeholders, families, and individuals who constantly support a global bilingual community in addressing the challenges that minority or minoritized languages must face to survive in today's society. Each bilingual speaker can contribute to the transmission of cultural values from one generation to the next. We hope this book will not only inspire more scientific research, necessary to expand our knowledge of bilingualism, but also support and encourage public engagement activities by language experts: This is what the Bilingualism Matters centre does at an international level.

The authors would like to thank Mirko Grimaldi who originally proposed the Italian book series "Il cervello linguistico" and made it possible for us to write the Italian version of this book.

1 WHO IS BILINGUAL?

Chapter Objectives

- Learn about the simultaneous or consecutive exposure to two languages and the stages of bilingualism;
- Examine the nature of codemixing and linguistic transfer;
- Explore how the bilingual brain works differently than the monolingual brain;
- Discuss the linguistic, cognitive, and socio-cognitive benefits of bilingualism across the life span and why it is important to learn more than one language in adulthood.

1.1 The Stages of Bilingualism

The regular use of more than one language is a widespread skill in society. Increased migration, the prevalence of research being published in English, foreign language learning, and more generally, the mobility of people and ideas, have contributed to an upsurge in bi-/multilingualism. Today, more than half of the world's population is estimated to be bilingual or multilingual. The European Commission (2016) found that around two-thirds of working-aged adults in the European Union (EU) knew at least one foreign language, about 21 percent defined themselves as trilingual (i.e., speaking two languages in addition to their first language, L1), and 8 percent said that they know three or more languages in addition to their first.

So, what exactly does it mean to be bilingual? Is this a phenomenon applicable to anyone as described above, or are speakers who only have a native or very advanced proficiency in two or more languages considered bilingual? The term **bilingualism** is often adopted loosely in everyday communication to refer to anyone who knows two languages or two linguistic **varieties**. In truth, many factors contribute to being bilingual, and we will see in the upcoming chapters that the way a language is learned and used varies considerably, both between communities and individual speakers.

Throughout this book, we will view bilingualism based on the *use* of languages and on the *situations* in which the brain is "juggling" languages. Thus, a person who knows more than one language and uses them to communicate is considered a bilingual, even if she does not have native-like proficiency in both languages. This definition is deliberately uncategorical. As we will discuss in Chapter 3, bilingualism is determined by the regular use of two languages, rather than by the level of competence achieved. For example, if an individual habitually speaks Hindi and a regional dialect spoken in India, or if she lives in India and speaks Hindi at school, at work, and during social activities, but her family speaks another language at home, she is considered a bilingual – her brain is constantly managing two languages and switching from one to the other. Bilingualism therefore does not only describe those who have a similar proficiency in the two languages and who speak both at the same level, but also to those who have a dominant language yet use the other in specific circumstances. Furthermore, the term bilingual can refer to adults who learn a second (L2) or third (L3) language, without having been exposed to it as a child, and who use it effectively in communicative situations. All of these variations of bilingualism are based on speakers' experiences, and they offer a unique opportunity to explore the effects of language learning on the brain. The various types of bilingualisms also allow us to ask questions about the neurobiology of language that involve cultural, social, and environmental factors. In practice, speaking more than one language can provide communicative and cognitive skills, even if an individual does not have native-like proficiency.

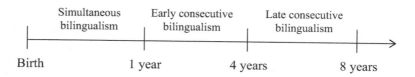

Figure 1.1 Stages of childhood bilingualism based on age of exposure to both languages.

From a scientific point of view, however, we need to fully describe the different stages of bilingualism. And to do this, we must identify and test the many variables that are essential to understand this phenomenon. These variables, which we will begin to discuss next, will accompany us along our journey into the bilingual brain.

To better define bilingualism, the first concept we should examine is **age of acquisition**, that is, the moment one first is exposed to a language. It is possible to become bilingual even in adulthood. However, as we will see, learning a language as an adult can lead to different stages of development and degrees of competence. With respect to age of acquisition, an important distinction that is reported in scientific research is between early and late bilingualism (see Figure 1.1). Early bilingualism has been studied extensively and involves learning more than one language from birth or within the first years of life. We can further classify early bilinguals as either simultaneous or consecutive bilinguals. A **simultaneous bilingual** is an individual who has learned more than one language in parallel since birth. An **early consecutive bilingual,** on the other hand, is one who has learned more than one language during childhood, but not from birth. Consecutive bilingualism can therefore affect different stages of childhood: if an L2 is introduced after the age of 4 but before the onset of puberty (say around 8 years of age), we refer to this as **late consecutive bilingualism.**

However, it is important to keep in mind that these age ranges and bilingual classifications are simply estimates; the unique experiences and different patterns of exposure to each of the two (or more) languages can give rise to several individual differences. Furthermore, it is not rare to find individuals who learn an L2 well into adulthood yet attain proficiency levels on par with their native-speaking counterparts (Paradis, 2011). We often refer to these individuals as **late adult**

bilinguals. These individuals are particularly important for studying the bilingual brain because it has often been claimed that the reduction of brain plasticity in adulthood is one of the causes of having poorer language learning outcomes as we age. In the strictest sense, calling individuals who have learned an L2 as adults *bilinguals* may seem incorrect. Thus, in the case of late bilinguals, it is appropriate to distinguish between those who are still learning an L2 and those who use both languages, if not in a balanced way, at least on a regular basis. This is because for many years it was believed that the biological period presumed to be available for language learning (the so-called **critical period**) is limited, and that after puberty, the linguistic functioning of the brain is somewhat different in L2 or L3 learning (Johnson & Newport, 1989). However, recent research shows that languages can be learned in adulthood to very high levels.

We also know that over the course of life, an L2 can become more dominant and cause changes in the first language. This has been demonstrated in studies on **language attrition**, that is, the phenomenon by which the L2 modifies the first (Sorace, 2011; Schmid & Köpke, 2019). Although many researchers adopt the term **second language acquisition** to refer to the process leading to bilingualism for adolescents and adults, in more recent research, the term bilingualism is preferred even for speakers who are not equally proficient in both languages but who make use of both languages on a regular basis. This is because – as we will also see in Chapter 4 – the brain may undergo morphological and functional changes due to language learning even well into adulthood.

Although adults can achieve near-native proficiency in an L2, learning two languages from an early age can have significant advantages, and therefore it makes no sense, as we will see in Chapter 6, to wait for the child to attain a certain level of competency in one language before exposing them to another. On the contrary, restricting exposure to an L2 in the most receptive period fails to exploit the many advantages of bilingual learning during these early years. In Chapter 2, we will see that **phonology** can benefit from early exposure to an L2. Vocabulary and pragmatic competence, on the other hand, are acquired almost continuously over the course of life and can change considerably with age. This is because the various domains of linguistic competence have different sensitive periods with unique characteristics. For instance, throughout our lives, we do not continuously learn and relearn the grammar or sounds of our languages, but it is not uncommon to acquire new words along the way or to find ourselves in new communicative environments.

Bilingualism Matters

A Bilingual Family: A Different Language Profile for Each Family Member

To illustrate the terminology presented thus far, let's take an example of a family of two parents and two daughters who move to a country where a language other than their mother tongue is spoken. One of the girls is 6 years old, the other is 8 months old, and they both have only been exposed to one language up until the move. The older girl, who is now learning an L2 in the prepubertal phase, represents a case of consecutive bilingualism. The younger girl, on the other hand, falls into the category of simultaneous bilingualism since the two languages will share a large part of the acquisition process during the critical period. On the contrary, both parents have an opportunity to acquire an L2 in their adulthood and therefore, if they have sufficient opportunity to practice both languages, they will become late bilinguals.

After a few years, it is possible that changes in language competence will happen for each member of the family. When parents practice the L2 regularly, they demonstrate that doing so is an active option that can be chosen when needed. The two girls will need to keep practicing both languages, and it is possible that their exposure to the family language will come mainly from family members. It is important at this stage to support their learning by offering exposure to the L1 with as much **input** from a variety of speakers as possible. Exposure to more varieties of the language will help to acquire cultural and linguistic features more fully.

1.2   Bilingualism and Codemixing

Bilingual speakers have the seemingly astonishing skill of switching from one language to another almost effortlessly. This observation is especially surprising in very young children who are still acquiring, or have yet to acquire, sophisticated cognitive reasoning skills. Although bilinguals distinguish between the two linguistic systems, they often tend to mix them and therefore show interference between one language and another. In the past, **codemixing**, such as inserting a word of a different language into a sentence or starting a sentence in one language and continuing it in another, was viewed as evidence for causing confusion in bilinguals' brains and for the inability to separate two languages in one mind. However, several studies have shown that for bilinguals, codemixing adheres to very precise linguistic and situational rules. In an experiment by Genesee et al. (1995), the amount of codemixing spoken by a bilingual adult was manipulated in a conversation with a child. The adult speech either included very little language mixing or a significant amount. The findings showed that the child adapted to the communicative situation, codemixing less when the adult did so less and more if the adult frequently codemixed. From the point of view of linguistic (syntactic) rules, it is not surprising that a bilingual can start a sentence in one language and end it in another. Nonetheless, very precise rules of mixing have been observed that suggest that bilinguals tend to follow the constraints of their languages. For example, an English-Portuguese bilingual might produce the sentence in (1) but it would be difficult for them to say something as in (2). This is because the words *some* and *rice*, as a constituent, form the object of *cooked* and thus, have a strong grammatical connection that is difficult to break apart with a language switch.

(1)   Esta manhã eu   cozinhei some rice.

(2)   Esta manhã eu   cozinhei some arroz.
        'This morning I have cooked   some rice.'

In general, codemixing is circumscribed to situations of interaction or to linguistic properties, as well as in the case of **transfer**, in which characteristics of one language affect the other. For example, it is possible that an English-Spanish bilingual makes some errors with grammatical gender in Spanish because English words are not always marked as such. So, you may hear him say (3) or (4), both of which are incorrect (*).

(3)   * La   chico   ha   caído
        * The.fem   boy.masc   has   fallen

(4)   * La   chica   está   cansado
         * The.fem   girl.fem   is   tired.masc

In Italian, on the other hand, grammatical gender is present in all relevant words, as shown in each word in (5) except for the verb è (third person singular of *essere*, 'to be').

(5)   La   ragazza   alta   è   cresciuta.
         The.fem   girl.fem   tall.fem has   grown.fem
         "The tall girl has grown."

The examples of transfer in (3)–(5) demonstrate the operations the brain unconsciously executes with language. Another linguistic phenomenon that occurs differently in languages is the possibility of not pronouncing the subject of a verb, as shown in Greek in (6). These languages, also including, Hindi, Italian, Portuguese, Spanish, among others, are known as pro-drop languages.

(6)   Βλέπεις   εκείνο   το   κούτσουρο
         See.2s   that   the   dog
         'You see that dog.'

Studies on English-Italian bilingual children show that, although bilingual children know that the subject can be omitted in Italian, they nonetheless make extensive use of subject pronouns as they would in English. For instance, based on the English gloss in (7), which requires the overt use of *he* as the subject of *will come*, English-Italian bilinguals may produce a sentence like in (7). An Italian monolingual[1] speaker would rarely specify *lui* as in (7) and would prefer not to verbalize it as was shown in (7) (Serratrice et al., 2004; Sorace et al., 2009). *Lui* in this sentence would normally be interpreted as referring to someone other than Gianni and therefore, bilinguals in this case introduce more ambiguity in the sentence.

(7)   Gianni   ha   detto   che   lui   verrà   domani
         Gianni   has   said   that   he.subj come.fut.3s   tomorrow.
         'Gianni has said that he will come tomorrow.'

---

[1] Throughout the book, the term "monolingual" is used to refer to individuals who are closer to the monolingual end of the bilingual continuum.

1.3 The Monolingual vs. Bilingual Debate

So far, we have defined the stages of bilingualism and have emphasized that an individual can be bilingual even when learning an L2 as an adult or making predictable language mixes. Before proceeding further, it is important to understand that bilinguals are not the sum of two monolingual speakers in one, nor should they be compared to monolinguals of each of the two languages (Grosjean, 1998). This belief often leads to an erroneous perception of the language abilities of bilinguals, who often feel that they are less proficient than monolinguals. And, in many circumstances, especially in educational settings, bilinguals feel that their bilingualism is ignored and undervalued. However, to researchers in bilingualism, the presence of a large population of bilingual speakers is a unique opportunity to discuss new topics that would not have otherwise emerged, such as the ability to learn languages, the possibility of using different language systems in various circumstances, and the facility to develop metalinguistic competence due to the comparisons that the brain makes between languages. But above all, bilingualism allows us to examine the influence that a varied and rich linguistic input has on the brain in its various cognitive abilities.

It is interesting to note that many aspects of bilingualism derive from the fact that the input of a monolingual speaker is often much more homogeneous than that of a bilingual speaker, although monolinguals use different registers of their language. Bilinguals are often exposed to diverse input in both languages, produced, for example, by a variety of speakers who may find themselves in one of many stages of language acquisition or attrition.

Several indices have been developed to measure the effects of input on linguistic development in bilinguals. The most common way is calculated by simply subtracting the number of years a bilingual has been exposed to a language from his age. In the example of the family presented earlier, the 6-year-old girl, who had never been exposed to the L2 before arriving in the new country, would be quite unbalanced when using this index: 6 for the native language minus 0 for the new language = 6. It is very likely that after a few years of living and going to school in the new country, the girl's L2 will become more dominant than her L1, but according to an index of 6, her first language should still be more dominant.

This suggests, first, that the traditional index may not be specific enough. In Chapter 6, we will present refined indices that dynamically and cumulatively consider the quantity and quality of input over time. These measures are therefore more appropriate for examining the effects of linguistic input. Secondly, it highlights the fact that language dominance is not a stable concept, but rather a dynamic process that differs from one individual to the next based on their unique language experiences. For example, in a study by Flege et al. (2002), the researchers examined the effects of age of arrival to Canada on language use and dominance among Italian-English bilinguals. The results showed that even speakers who arrived later as adults tended to perceive the L2 as dominant, given their constant use of it in their everyday lives. Therefore, linguistic experience – and as we shall see, cognitive factors – of a bilingual speaker clearly differentiate them from monolinguals. In sum, due to the changes that bilingualism causes in various stages of life and because of the greater variability of the input to which bilingual speakers are exposed, they cannot be viewed as two monolingual speakers in one.

1.4 Why Is It Important to Talk About a Bilingual Brain?

Research on the neural bases of language initiated because of new tools in neuroscience. Initially, this body of work was limited to examining monolingual speakers and did not consider the effects that bilingualism has on the brain. From a cerebral point of view, it was assumed that the knowledge of one language, and therefore, its neural representation, was not modified by the presence of an L2 or L3 and that it was sufficient to study the brain of a monolingual speaker to understand how the language(s) in general was/were processed in the brain.

However, the last twenty years of research has adapted a neuroscientific perspective that favors a more ecological study of languages, the brain, and its functions – a view which reflects the way we really use languages. By enhancing the study of bilingualism during neuroimaging experiments with actual *bilingual* participants, we have gained a greater understanding of how language is organized in the brain. And for the study of the bilingual brain, new cross-disciplinary intersections such as linguistics and neuroscience have produced refined models that can characterize the neural properties of languages. In Chapters 3 and 4, we will discuss in detail neuroimaging studies examining areas of brain activity. We will see that languages are all processed in the same way by monolinguals and that there is no difference with respect to how Spanish or Chinese, for example, are organized in the brain. In other words, at the phonological, morphological, syntactic, and pragmatic levels, the respective brain and temporal areas that are activated are very similar regardless of the language in question. However, differences *do* emerge if we measure the sensitive variables for bilingualism, which we discussed above, namely language proficiency, the age at which an individual is first exposed to the language, and the quantity and quality of linguistic input.

In a seminal study by Perani et al. (1996), the researchers used **positron emission tomography (PET)** to identify a qualitative difference between the activation of specific areas of the left hemisphere while listening to stories in the mother tongue (Italian), in the L2 learned as adults (English), and in an unknown language (Japanese). PET is a brain imaging technique that uses a harmless radioactive drug to trace and measure changes in functional processes in the brain. In this study, brain activity while listening in the mother tongue was more intense and uniform than the language learned later. The study, however, was limited to speakers who had learned English as adults and thus did not explore whether the differential activity level in the L2 was due to proficiency level or age of exposure. These variables were instead considered by Perani et al. (1998) in which the researchers tested Italian adults who learned English after the age of 10 and Spanish-Catalan bilinguals who used both languages on a regular basis and acquired them before the age of 4. The findings suggested that the regular use of the languages, rather than the age of acquisition, was more crucial for language learning in adulthood.

In sum, new horizons in language neuroscience are challenging the idea that languages can only be acquired by children. It seems more plausible that the differences between speakers, found, for example, in word naming tasks in the L2, are potentially related to linguistic competence rather than age of exposure. Neuroimaging techniques, among other things, can show us how the brain recruits areas predisposed to language processing and other areas, such as the prefrontal regions associated with cognitive control that generally would not fit into the brain network of a speaker with high competence (Perani & Abutalebi, 2005). There are also some conflicting neuroimaging data that must be interpreted in the context of a coherent language network in the brain. Some studies have shown that depending on the linguistic task selected, there is less activity in temporoparietal areas for less proficient bilinguals than for highly proficient bilinguals. Moreover, it seems that language experience and especially practice (i.e., factors that can change even in a short period) can produce important brain changes (Perani et al., 2003). In Chapter 4, we will review this expanding body of research and see that in general, the findings support brain plasticity – even in adulthood – that adapts with practice, at least for certain aspects of language acquisition.

Now, in addition to the differences linked to linguistic factors (e.g., sensitivity to phonological or grammatical factors) or to environmental factors (e.g., exposure or age of acquisition), one of the most fascinating discoveries that research in bilingualism has offered is that being bilingual seems to modify the brain even outside of the domain of language itself and has consequences both for cognition and personal health.

1.5   The Benefits of Bilingualism

A unique attribute of bilingual speakers is that they have a heightened understanding of how language works. Bilingual children are intuitively interested in the structure and functioning of languages and they unconsciously notice the differences and similarities between them. Parents often observe how bilingual children "play" with languages, for example, by creating new words that do not exist in one language but that sound familiar in the other, imitating different accents, or creating predictable mistakes in one language. Part of these important metalinguistic skills is that bilingual speakers develop a greater ability to distinguish between the shape and meaning of words, naturally sensing that a meaning, such as the concept of *dog*, can have different linguistic forms in various languages: *chien* in French, *kalb* in Arabic, *perro* in Spanish, and 狗 ("gǒu") in Mandarin.

In reality, there are two words (one in each language) for every concept in the bilingual brain – for an Arabic-Spanish bilingual, *kalb* and *perro* both refer to a dog. This increases the ability to reflect on language and stimulates the acquisition of vocabulary within each language. For instance, as we will see in Chapter 2, bilinguals may acquire synonyms easier, even though they are more easily avoided in the early stages of language learning. Furthermore, because of these sharpened metalinguistic skills, research has shown that in some cases, bilingual children learn to read before monolinguals. This early reading ability, which has been found in particular in learning alphabetic writing systems, derives from the fact that bilinguals are better at recognizing the systematic correspondence between written letters and spoken sounds (Bialystok & Herman, 1999). Their decoding mechanisms while reading are more transparent, although this may be connected to having literacy in the other language as well. It has also been reported that metalinguistic awareness of language structure has a positive effect on learning a third or fourth language, as is often observed by both families and teachers (Abu Rabia & Sanitsky, 2010).

Putting aside the linguistic domain for now, there are other potential benefits of bilingualism that are connected to general cognition, and in particular, to some aspects of **executive control** that regulate attention mechanisms. Research has shown that compared to age-matched monolinguals, bilinguals often have an advantage in laboratory experiments in which rapid switching from one task to another is required, when interfering factors must be ignored, and when selective attention is involved. As we will discuss in Chapter 3, some of these tasks measure the speed and accuracy of reacting to a stimulus. These advantages are not temporary, but rather persist into adulthood, as has been found in adults who have grown up speaking two languages from childhood (Bialystok et al., 2008). But why is there a link between bilingualism and executive control? From the brain activity of bilinguals, the main hypothesis is that both languages are constantly active in the brain. In a practical sense, the brain always keeps the possibility open to call on and use any language it knows. The obvious problem is that we cannot speak two languages at the same time. Therefore, bilingual speakers seem to develop an inhibition mechanism that allows them to keep the two languages separate in order to limit the language not being used from interfering with the target language – all while keeping it actively available to some degree. The exception to this is **bimodal bilingualism,** which refers to the regular use of a signed language and an oral language (Emmorey et al., 2008).

So, for bilinguals, the prolonged experience of inhibiting one language when speaking the other strengthens control mechanisms that are utilized in other activities requiring attention and executive control. Consequently, this improves the ability to perform multiple cognitive tasks simultaneously or in rapid succession. Some studies suggest that these cognitive advantages are maintained into old age and can protect bilinguals from some of the typical phenomena associated with aging, such as decline in cognitive functioning (Bialystok et al., 2008). It is important to note that if the benefits of bilingualism derive from the constant practice of inhibiting one language while the other is being used, then this should happen in all bilinguals, regardless of which languages they speak. Therefore, there are no languages that are "better" for the brain than others. In fact, cognitive advantages have also been reported for bilinguals who speak minority and regional languages such as Sardinian (Garraffa et al., 2015; Garraffa et al., 2017).

Another little-known benefit of bilingualism is the greater and earlier awareness that other people have a different perspective than their own. The phenomenon of **decentralized cognition** is often defined in cognitive and developmental psychology in the context of **theory of mind.** It has been reported in some studies that the ability to see the point of view of others is achieved by bilingual children about a year earlier than monolingual ones. This advantage seems to be linked to the bilinguals' constant practice with monitoring the linguistic competence of their listeners in order to better adapt their language choices to the particular person with whom they are speaking (e.g., whether the listener is a monolingual of Language A, monolingual of Language B, or a bilingual of A and B (Kovács, 2009).

Finally, more recent research on the effects of bilingualism on cognition has found that **decision-making** behavior, or the way we make decisions, is conditioned by the language in which the decision is made. Some experiments have shown that humans are less sensitive to emotions if processing information in a foreign language (Costa et al., 2014). In other words, our choices are influenced less by things like happiness or nervousness when we are using the L2. Interestingly, the effects of a foreign language on decision-making are limited to situations that involve emotional factors. If, on the other hand, the situation has no emotional relevance, decision-making seems to be no different in the L1 or L2. The conclusion of these studies is that the effect of making decisions in an L2 reduces the influence of emotions and sharpens the focus on the choices at hand.

Bilingualism Matters

Cognitive and Linguistics Advantages of Minority Languages

Most research on the benefits of bilingualism has reported on speakers of "global languages" such as Spanish, Chinese, or English. Some researchers are now addressing the issue of whether bilingualism involving global vs. minority languages is a modulating factor of the benefit of bilingualism. In principle there is no reason for us to believe that the brain discriminates between languages based on the number of speakers or the social prestige of a language.

It is important that research in bilingualism include studies on languages that are often considered dialects and minoritized, as this is crucial in better defining the advantages for the bilingual brain. Some research has been conducted on language varieties spoken in Italy in the Sardinian Island where the local languages are practiced and passed on to the new generations. The language is more diffused in the central part of Sardinia, where people are conversing in Sardinian and using the dominant language, Italian, mostly for formal communication.

In a study by Garraffa et al. (2017), adult fluent Sardinian-Italian speakers were reported to have enhanced verbal memory (i.e., a stronger ability to recall a list of numbers/facts/words) compared to monolingual Italian adults living in the same area. Moreover, while this same group of bilinguals had no formal postsecondary education, they showed better memory skills compared to educated individuals living in the same area but not using Sardinian regularly. The findings suggest that bilingualism with an oral language can benefit verbal memory, due to the unique oral medium and the consequent need of memorizing. Many regional/local languages in the world have no writing system or have little use of reading and writing. Unfortunately, this often classifies the language as less prestigious, as it is not represented in literature or news. Although having a writing system is extremely important, bilinguals whose language does not have a writing system can develop enhanced cognitive abilities such as memory skills.

Other studies on regional languages have been conducted on Gaelic, a language spoken in Scotland (e.g., Garraffa et al., 2020). The studies often involve children studying at Gaelic medium education (GME) schools who are learning how to read and write in both Gaelic and English. While there are not many examples of schools across the world promoting biliteracy of a regional language, the GME schools in Scotland offer Gaelic as the primary language and source for literacy and English as a modern language subject. In the study by Dickson et al. (2021) the authors compared English reading abilities among students from the GME system and monolingual English students in non-GME schools. The findings showed that English literacy among the children in GME schools was on par with that of English monolingual children in non-GME schools. Furthermore, by the last years of education in the GME schools, the individuals outperform their monolingual counterparts in English reading. These positive findings about biliteracy are crucial for many families and schools which are considering education in more than one language.

1.6   Why Learn a New Language?

The outcomes of learning a language, especially as adults, generally reveal significant individual differences such that some individuals manage to attain a very high proficiency in the languages while others may struggle. At times, one may wonder if it is worth trying to learn a new language, or whether it would be enough to exercise the brain with less complex activities. The answer is not so much whether it is better to start learning a language, say after the age of 40, to do at least one Sudoku per day, or to work on cognitive training programs. Research is showing that what is important for the development of a healthy brain is to keep the brain trained with complex and stimulating activities, which can progress in complexity. However, it is even better if these activities entail social interaction (Valenzuela & Sachdev, 2009). Accordingly, learning a language seems to be the ideal activity that meets the criteria for the development of a healthy brain, as suggested by studies on aging. Learning an L2 is certainly not the only activity beneficial for maintaining a health brain; however, because languages are often widely available within one's region or country (e.g., minority languages and regional varieties are a significant asset), and because traveling is more available than it was before, doing so can improve daily activities that can be integrated into lifestyles.

There are still many questions about whether the manner of language learning or the environment in which a language is learned can have additional influences on the human brain. A recent study on a group of adults attending an intensive language course showed improved attention control after only one week of language learning compared to individuals who had either attended other intensive activities or simply maintained their normal routines (Bak et al., 2016). These findings suggest that engaging in language learning pays off quickly, with visible effects at any age that are maintained over time if practiced regularly. We will return to these issues in Chapter 4.

Research addressing how to lead a healthy lifestyle now includes learning a language. The impact of language learning on the health and well-being of individuals is a fascinating subject that presents new perspectives on why it is important to learn languages. In countries with a large number of monolinguals, such as in the United Kingdom where English reigns for its global usefulness, foreign language education is undervalued, resulting in a significant reduction in the number of people who learn languages compared to other countries. This is because social benefits are associated with knowing the global language and because research has not yet been able to massively inform society about the benefits of bilingualism for cognition and that these benefits are the same for *every language* including minority and regional languages.

Summary

In this chapter, we have discussed how to define bilingualism based on the actual use of the language and not so much on the level of proficiency or the age of acquisition of the languages. Bilingualism has been defined as a continuum on which speakers are able to move as a result of their exposure to and practice with the languages. Throughout the chapter, we have introduced the key terms in bilingualism that help us to more accurately characterize the nature of speakers of two or more languages. We also discussed the phenomenon of codeswitching as a rule-governed process, along with examples from different languages. The chapter also presented some of the differences between bilingual and monolingual competence, followed by a brief look at the cognitive benefits of bilingualism. In reporting evidence from empirical research about the bilingual brain, we offered considerations about the benefits of language learning for healthy aging across the life span – regardless of the social prestige attached to the languages.

Discussion Topics

1. Bilingualism has been presented as a dynamic process across the life span. Define two or three factors that can affect bilingualism.
2. Bilingual speakers often mix languages, generating sentences in one language with inserted words from another language. Define what codemixing is and provide two or three examples that show how it is rule governed.
3. It has been argued that bilingualism can have benefits outside of the language domain. Provide two or three examples of nonlinguistic domains that can benefit from bilingualism.
4. Bilingualism can be a positive resource at any age. Briefly describe why bilingualism matters, particularly in adulthood and later years of life.
5. Discuss whether the benefits associated with bilingualism depend on their global or social status.
6. Discuss some evidence for the proposal of a bilingual brain.
7. Describe decentralized cognition and its relationship with bilingualism.

2 THE DEVELOPMENT OF TWO LANGUAGES
Phonology, Lexicon, and Morphosyntax

Chapter Objectives

- Analyze how languages are acquired in bilingual contexts;
- Explore how phonological competence develops in monolingual and bilingual children;
- Discuss advantages and disadvantages during bilingual lexical development;
- Highlight differences and similarities in the acquisition of morpho-syntactic skills among monolinguals and bilinguals; and
- Learn about the important benefits of early exposure to two languages simultaneously.

2.1 The Acquisition of Two Languages

Language acquisition is one of the most extraordinary human experiences: even if we often take it for granted, it is fascinating to note how children in a few years are able to master a system as complex as that of their L1 in a completely natural and innate way, effortlessly and, above all, without the need for explicit instruction or being directly corrected by adults.

However, the memories we have about learning foreign languages, especially in primary and secondary education, are generally very different. The mere fact that we are talking about learning, rather than acquisition, immediately gives the impression that it is a more challenging procedure, generally linked to explicit teaching in a formal (e.g., classroom) context. Learning an L2 in this case takes much longer than learning the mother tongue and can lead to very different outcomes: even if achieving optimal competence is certainly possible, it is sometimes the case that learning stops at lower proficiency levels, due to a variety of factors.

Perhaps this is why there is a tendency to be prejudiced about the development of two or more languages in bilingual children. As we will see in Chapter 6, parents often wonder whether it is too early to expose children to multiple languages from birth, and whether there is the risk of confusing them. In reality, as we will see, the brain, especially that of infants and young children, is perfectly capable of handling two or more languages, without confusion, in a completely natural way that is similar to that of monolinguals.

In this chapter, we will focus precisely on the mechanisms involved in bilingual development at the phonological, lexical, and morphosyntactic level. These language domains have rapidly and relatively recently become the subject of numerous scientific studies. The main research question to be answered concerns whether two languages have the same or separate linguistic systems in the bilingual brain. It is evident that this question is of crucial importance to language acquisition theory and, more generally, to the human language faculty, as it allows us to establish whether humans have an innate predisposition to become bi/multilingual or whether monolingualism is the default option and multilingualism comes at the cost of slower cognitive development. In fact, if we were born to be monolingual, we would expect an initial confusion in children exposed to two languages simultaneously, which would demonstrate the time and effort needed to separate the two language systems. If, on the other hand, humans were predisposed to acquire more than one language at the same time, one would expect that simultaneous bilinguals have similar rates of development as their monolingual peers, without confusion or consistent setbacks.

According to the **Unitary Language System Hypothesis** (Volterra & Taeschner, 1978), bilinguals develop a single linguistic system, that is, a unified grammar that includes words from both languages. They later begin to develop two different lexical systems

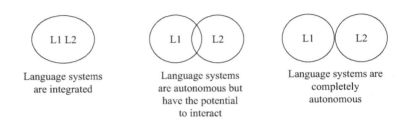

Figure 2.1 Unitary Language System Hypothesis showing integration, interaction, and separation of linguistic systems.

but continue to apply the same syntactic rules from the dominant language to both languages. Finally, in a third stage, two distinct grammatical systems emerge in which there is full differentiation between the two languages (Figure 2.1). After around 3 years of age, bilinguals typically show linguistic behavior similar to age-matched monolinguals. Volterra and Taeschner offered support for their hypothesis by analyzing the frequency of codemixing (as discussed in Chapter 1) used by bilinguals, which they, unfortunately erroneously, interpreted as a symptom of confusion and the inability to distinguish the two languages.

Contrary to what this hypothesis predicts, it has been widely demonstrated that bilinguals develop two independent language systems from their initial exposure to two languages. This differentiation process is observable in infants well before they begin to speak. The two languages are nevertheless connected to each other and can dynamically influence one another in over the course of life.

2.2   The Acquisition of Phonology

The first challenge that infants who are exposed to two languages will face is in the domain of **phonology**. They must correctly discriminate the two language systems by distinguishing the sounds in one language from sounds in the other. This task may seem relatively easy for consecutive bilinguals whose phonological system in one language is sufficiently developed to allow them to identify sounds from a new language. However, for a newborn, whose sound and lexical systems have not yet developed, discriminating sounds in one language from the other is no trivial challenge. Without the ability to rely on lexical information to distinguish the two languages, simultaneous bilingual infants will therefore have to make use of **prosodic cues,** such as intonation, accent, and rhythmic structure of the two languages, while learning the two sound systems.

From birth, numerous studies on language acquisition have shown that infants are able to recognize their L1 through prosodic information (i.e., melodic aspects that characterize rhythmic and accentual structure). Results from studies using the high-amplitude sucking method, a technique that measures infants' sucking reflexes, are particularly interesting. Typically, infants demonstrate more vigorous sucking when they feel new or pleasant stimuli. Just a few days after birth, babies show that they are sensitive to their L1 and can distinguish it from languages that belong to a different **rhythmic class** or have different prosodic properties. For instance, a study conducted by Mehler and colleagues (1988) found that at only 4 days of age, French infants were able to distinguish Italian, a language belonging to the same rhythmic class as their L1 French, from English, a language belonging to a different class. This skill is refined further and by around 4 or 5 months, babies can discriminate between their L1 and languages belonging to the same rhythmic class or those with similar prosodic characteristics.

While these abilities were widely found in monolingual children as early as 1990, more recently it has been reported that bilinguals, rather than being confused by simultaneous exposure to two different language systems, follow the same developmental stages as their monolingual peers. In other words, the bilingual children show sensitivity to both languages and immediately succeed at distinguishing them correctly from other unfamiliar languages. A study by Byers-Heinlein et al. (2010), for example, compared few-day-old babies born to English monolingual mothers and English-Tagalog bilingual mothers who had used both languages during pregnancy. In the study, the infants listened to sentences uttered in each of the two languages. The infants born to English monolingual mothers showed a marked preference for English, demonstrating the fact that they were able to distinguish the two language systems. The infants born to the bilingual mothers, on the other hand, expressed an interest in both languages, while being able to differentiate them, suggesting that a sensitivity to the two languages had already been developed prenatally. Similarly, Bosch and Sebastián-Gallés (2001) conducted a study which showed that Spanish-Catalan bilingual babies were able to distinguish between these two phonologically and rhythmically similar languages by the age of 4 months.

In addition to phonological sensitivity, visual factors such as lip movements, gestures, and facial expressions appear to be important in guiding linguistic differentiation. In fact, both bilingual and monolingual babies are able to distinguish their L1 from an unfamiliar language simply by watching videos without audio in which people speaking different languages are shown in the foreground (Weikum et al., 2007). However, this ability appears to be stronger for bilingual babies, who at the age of 8 months are able to discriminate even two languages never heard before more effectively than monolingual babies. Further evidence of these findings has come from research in neuroscience: Ramírez et al. (2016) used **magnetoencephalography** (**MEG**), a functional neuroimaging technique which uses magnetic fields produced by electrical currents in the brain to map neural activity, and found that 11-month-old English-Spanish bilinguals had a clear ability to discriminate between the two languages.

As for sound discrimination, we know that from birth, all children develop the ability to distinguish phonemic contrasts (e.g., the sounds /b/ and /p/ in the words "bat" and "pat" create a contrast that is strong enough to distinguish one word from the other). In bilingual children, this ability is slower during the first year of life to make room for greater sensitivity to sounds in two languages. Again, while the rate of acquiring this ability may be reduced for bilinguals, they still follow the same trajectory as monolinguals and arrive at a native mastery of sounds in the languages to which they are exposed.

Monolingual and bilingual babies show other similar stages of development and timing. For example, both populations begin to **babble** by six months, producing well-formed syllables composed of consonants and vowels (e.g., *lalala, mamama, bababa*). Although the characteristics of the first "babbles" are universal, in the following months, they begin to show characteristics that are specific to the child's L1. An interesting study by Maneva and Genesee (2002) considered the case of a bilingual child whose mother spoke to him in English and whose father spoke to him in French. The research showed that the baby's babbling, monitored from 10 to 15 months, showed distinct characteristics in terms of the number of syllables and syllabic structure that depended on the interlocutor's language. The baby used typical sound characteristics of French when addressing his dad, and of English when speaking to his mom. Similar findings were reported by Poulin-Dubois and Goodz (2001), who found bilingual modalities in terms of phonological structure among a group of 12-month-old French-English bilinguals, confirming the differentiation of the two languages prior to the emergence of the first words.

Although there are similar developmental stages of phonological competence among monolingual and bilingual children, it must be noted that slight differences or delays are sometimes observed, both in receptive and productive language abilities. In a study by Bosch and Sebastián-Gallés (2003), Spanish-Catalan bilinguals showed delays on phonemic discrimination tasks, although these delays disappeared within a few months. As for production, however, a study by Fabiano-Smith and Barlow (2010) found that 3-year-old English-Spanish bilinguals produced slightly less accurate pronunciation than age-matched monolingual children, although this difference was within the normal range of phonetic repertoire among monolingual children. Nonetheless, these are negligible differences given that bilinguals are acquiring a sophisticated competence of *two* linguistic systems in the same time span as monolinguals. It is therefore a small price to pay considering the inestimable wealth that exposure to two languages from birth can bring. We know, in fact, that phonological competence, and in particular pronunciation, is the area that is most affected by age of exposure to an L2. As we have mentioned, the decline in the ability to discriminate sounds belonging to one language or another begins toward the age of 1 and continues in subsequent years, and by puberty, it is much more difficult to achieve a native accent.

In summary, these studies offer insight as to whether simultaneous exposure to two languages can create confusion or slow the linguistic development of children. The results clearly show that bilinguals use the same mechanisms of learning and prosodic and phonetic discrimination as monolinguals, suggesting that the differentiation of the two linguistic systems emerges very early in bilinguals.

Bilingualism Matters

When Should Exposure to Two Languages Happen?

One of the most common concerns expressed by caregivers is that simultaneous exposure to two languages from birth might be disruptive to their child's development. The fear that bilingualism may cause confusion and hinder children's development might lead caregivers to expose them to the L2 after a few years, once the L1 is already in place. As discussed in this chapter, scientific research actually shows that simultaneous bilinguals can perfectly handle the two (or more) languages to which they are exposed, and that they do not show marked delays or problems in the acquisition of their languages. The suggestion for bilingual families is then not to wait, but to opt for simultaneous exposure, which provides their children the opportunity to develop harmonic and similar language competence in both languages.

2.3 The Acquisition of Vocabulary

It is often mistakenly believed that simultaneous bilinguals have delays in vocabulary development. However, this is a false myth which is very important to dispel, given that late emergence of the first linguistic productions (after 24–30 months) can indicate the presence of a language disorder, as we will discuss more in detail in Chapter 5.

In reality, bilinguals produce their first words at the same time as monolinguals, around 12–13 months, and follow a similar pace of vocabulary development. One of the first studies conducted in this area was by Pearson et al. (1993) who compared both receptive and productive vocabulary of 8- to 30-month-old English monolinguals and English-Spanish bilinguals. The results showed similar developmental stages for the two groups. The findings also revealed that vocabulary comprehension in both English and Spanish for the bilingual group was similar to English for the monolinguals. As for production, however, the authors found that vocabulary was lower in bilinguals than in monolinguals when considering each of the two languages separately, although equivalent when considering the total vocabulary in both languages. Indeed, it is estimated that the lexicon of a monolingual child by age 3 includes about 800–900 words and that the lexicon of a bilingual peer typically has the same overall amount considering the two languages together. Furthermore, it must be observed that the size of the vocabulary varies according to the amount of use in the two languages, with the dominant, more frequently used languages having richer lexicons.

This is a point that must be carefully examined: there are many studies, in fact, which have highlighted significant differences in the breadth of the vocabulary of both bilingual children and adults. A study by Bialystok and colleagues (2010) administered a receptive vocabulary test to 1,738 monolingual and bilingual children between 3 and 10 years old. In the test, the children were shown four images and were asked to point to one that corresponded to a word they heard (e.g., the child was to point to the image of a hand if she heard the word "hand"). The results showed that, in all age groups considered, bilinguals had a significantly lower receptive vocabulary in the language spoken by the monolinguals. However, differences were found only with domestic-related vocabulary (e.g., words such as "ladle" or "drying rack") but not for school-related vocabulary (e.g., words such as "astronaut" and "rectangle"). In other words, bilinguals tested in the language they use at school typically have the same knowledge about school-related words in that language as monolingual peers. They cannot, however, know domestic-related words to which they have never been exposed.

The findings from Bialystok et al.'s (2010) study present two interesting considerations: firstly, it suggests that bilinguals' lower receptive abilities in vocabulary does not have repercussions on their vocabulary in academic settings, given that lexical knowledge in this context is similar to that of monolinguals. Secondly, it highlights the fact that bilinguals' vocabulary is developed individually to meet their needs for using both languages. This finding aligns with predictions put forth in the Complementarity Principle (Grosjean, 2008), whereby bilinguals use their languages for different purposes in their lives and consequently, each language will be more or less specialized than the other in certain domains.

These aspects are completely natural and understandable and must be taken into account when evaluating bilinguals' vocabulary.

This is especially important if, as is generally the case, their performance is compared to monolinguals. For instance, for a bilingual child who is subjected to a standardized vocabulary test designed only for monolinguals (as unfortunately normally happens), it is highly probable that the child will demonstrate lower performance than the monolingual norm. This may consequently place or categorize them in an "at risk" range for a language disorder. Ignoring the vocabulary abilities in both languages can lead to serious misunderstandings and misdiagnoses of learning disorders, when in fact the child's bilingual development is perfectly normal.

When considering lexical development, it has been shown that bilinguals' two linguistic systems differ early and that, very early on, they acquire words in both languages that refer to the same concept. A Tagalog-English bilingual will know, for example, that the word "kutsara" and the English word "spoon" refer to the same object. Numerous studies have shown that bilinguals have translations of the same term into both languages as early as 8 months (Deuchar & Quay, 2000) and that the words they know in both languages by the age of 1.5 correspond to approximately 20–25 percent of their overall vocabulary (Nicoladis & Secco, 2000). Clearly, this would not be possible if the child had an integrated linguistic system in which a single word corresponded to a concept.

In an **eye-tracking** study, a method that allows researchers to record participants' eye movements as they process visual stimuli, Byers-Heinlein et al. (2017) presented images depicting two objects (e.g., a book and a dog) to 20-month-old English-French bilinguals. The participants were told, in either English or French, to look at one or the other image. But in this request, sometimes the target picture name was intentionally switched into the opposite language (e.g., "Look! Find the *chien*!") and sometimes it was the same language (e.g., "Look! Find the dog!"). The results revealed that the children, despite always being accurate in directing their gaze to the correct image, showed surprise and delayed responses when the language switch occurred. These findings suggest that the children first activated one of their languages (i.e., the one spoken by the interlocutor), and that the insertion of the other language created a processing cost that slowed down responses. If the two terms had been stored in one linguistic system, in fact, no cost could have been expected from one language to another.

Bilingual children are therefore consciously aware of the fact that words in both languages can correspond to the same concept. This leads them to develop better cognitive flexibility and more effective vocabulary learning strategies than those typically seen in monolingual children. This observation is reflected in various applications of the so-called Principle of Mutual Exclusivity (Markman & Wachtel, 1988) in which vocabulary learning is based on the creation of arbitrary associations between words heard and objects seen. Imagine a child learning a new word. Hearing their caregiver utter the word cat when seeing a cat, after a certain number of repetitions, the child will learn to associate the object with the sounds heard in the corresponding word. Although it may seem simple, this operation is quite complex: how does the child understand that the caregiver is referring to the animal itself, instead of to a part of it (e.g., the tail or paw), to one of its attributes (e.g., color or softness), or to an action that the cat is performing (e.g., meowing or purring)? The child thus finds himself in a situation similar to that described by Quine (1960) in his famous thought experiment of radical translation, in which he described the task of an ethnolinguist who met an Indigenous individual whose language he did not know. When the ethnolinguist heard the individual say *gavagai* as a rabbit passed by, he may have assumed that it referred to the animal, but it would only be a hypothesis that would then be verified and possibly corrected or modified with additional experience. To be able to juggle this complex task, the child must adopt **heuristics,** or simplification strategies: one of these shortcuts, as hypothesized by the Principle of Mutual Exclusivity, is that each object is initially associated with a single name. The observance of this principle was demonstrated in a simple experiment by Markman and Wachtel (1988) in which a group of 3- to 4-year-old children were presented with two objects, one familiar (e.g., a cup) and one unfamiliar (e.g., a fuse). The experimenter then asked the participant to perform an action with one of the two objects, using an invented word (e.g., "Give me the *pintire*"). The results indicated that the children consistently associated the new word with the unfamiliar object, for which they did not yet have a name.

Although the notion of mutual exclusivity helps children in constructing the mental lexicon, it can, like all heuristics, lead to errors. A typical consequence of its application lies in the difficulty that young

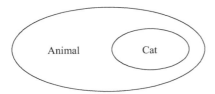

Figure 2.2 The relationship of hypernymy and hyponymy in the mental lexicon.

children often have in understanding the relationships of inclusion that characterize the hierarchical structure of the lexicon, such as **hypernyms** and **hyponyms**. The word *animal* and the word *cat*, in other words, cannot be considered on the same level, since all cats are animals, but not all animals are cats. So, animal is a hypernym, because it is hierarchically larger, and *cat* is a hyponym (see Figure 2.2) because it is a type of animal.

Young children often have difficulty understanding that a cat is both a cat and an animal. To acquire this type of hierarchical relationship, they must learn to avoid the Principle of Mutual Exclusivity, that is, they must learn that multiple words can correspond to the same referent.

The fact that bilinguals have a term in each of the two languages for the same subject is in itself a violation of this principle. It is possible that bilinguals are less compliant with the principle. Several studies have shown that heuristics are used consistently by monolinguals, who even at the age of 6 tend to attribute a word they do not know to an unfamiliar part or property of an object whose name they already know. In contrast, bilinguals appear to be much more flexible, relying on mutual exclusivity to a lesser extent than monolinguals (Davidson & Tell, 2005). This tendency is even absent in trilinguals, who accept without difficulty the fact that several words can refer to the same object (Byers-Heinlein & Werker, 2009).

The results of these studies underscore the presence of differences in lexical learning related to bi-/multilingualism, and in particular, in the role that linguistic experience plays in shaping and guiding language acquisition. Even though there are positive effects (i.e., flexibility and early understanding of the hierarchical nature of the mental lexicon) of avoiding the mutual exclusivity principle in the case of bi-/ multilinguals, we should also recognize that the use of this heuristic represents an effective "shortcut" which facilitates the path of lexical development. In fact, not being able to rely on this heuristic could make the task more challenging for bi-/multilinguals.

Bilingualism Matters

Lexical Competence in Bilinguals

Vocabulary knowledge is a challenging area for bilingual children. It is often the case that bilinguals know a word in one language, but do not know its translation equivalent, that is, the same word in the other language. Let's take the case of a Farsi L1 speaker who uses English purely for work reasons: her vocabulary in the professional field is richer in English, to the point that she would likely struggle to translate some of her work jargon into Farsi. On the contrary, she does not know the English translation of terms related to her family life, since this language is less frequently used in the home.

Every bilingual will have, at least once in their lives, an experience in which they find themselves talking about a topic in the "wrong" language and have difficulty finding the right words without having to retrieve them in the other language. This is a very common situation, which should not be a cause of concern, but should be seen as a consequence of bilinguals' specialized vocabulary reflecting their typical patterns of language use.

2.4   The Acquisition of Morphosyntax

In this section we will focus on the development of **morphology** and **syntax** in bilingual children. Morphological skills concern the ability to inflect words, for example by correctly conjugating a verb like *I read* vs. *he reads*, to pluralize a noun such as book vs. books, and to derive words from other words like the noun *worker* from the verb *to work*. Syntactic skills, on the other hand, involve the ability to combine these words into phrases and sentences, such as: *The worker reads books*.

Morphosyntactic development in bilinguals has been the subject of numerous studies that seek to better understand whether both grammatical systems of bilinguals develop to the same degree as monolinguals and whether there is interference between the two language systems (i.e., negative transfer effects). The results generally confirm that even with regard to grammatical competence, the development patterns of bilinguals and monolinguals are the same, indicating that bilinguals are able to acquire grammatical structures of two languages at the same time.

In particular, studies analyzing the first sentences produced by simultaneous bilinguals report that they are able to use structural properties specific to each language at an early stage. For instance, typically, monolingual French children acquire the verbal inflection toward the age of 2, whereas English monolinguals do so toward 3 years old, due to differences in the cognitive demands of the syntactic operations in the two languages. Paradis and Genesee (1996) observed that English-French bilinguals showed the same development rate as English and French monolinguals, acquiring, for example, the inflection of the verb in French by around age 2 followed by verb inflection in English at around age 3. The similarity between the English-French bilinguals and the monolinguals of both languages suggests that the two language systems develop in an autonomous way. Even in the context of producing structures such as negation and subject pronouns, that differ in the two languages bilinguals show the same acquisitional pattern as monolinguals in each language.

This does not mean, however, that the two linguistic systems should be considered separate entities. On the contrary, a certain degree of interaction between the two languages, especially at initial levels, has been reported in several studies. Döpke (1998), for example, studied the acquisition of verb position among simultaneous 2-year-old English-German bilinguals. English and German have the same word order in simple sentences, as exemplified in (8a) and (8b) in which the verb *to be* occurs after the subject (i.e., it occupies the second position). Their word order is different, however, in more complex sentences such as those in which an infinitive occurs at the end of the sentence in German (9a), whereas in English, it follows directly after the modal verb (9b).

(8a)   Die Sonne ist gelb.

(8b)   The sun   is   yellow.

(9a)   Ich kann Tennis spielen.

(9b)   I   can   tennis   play.
         "I can play tennis."

Döpke found that bilinguals go through a phase in which they do not respect this rule, producing ungrammatical sentences as in (10), which appears to follow English word order, rather than the grammatic target in (11).

(10)   *Ich möchte essen das.
          I   want   to eat this.

(11)   Ich möchte das essen.
         I   want   this to eat.
         "I want to eat this."

Since this type of error is not typically found in monolingual peers, it can be assumed that it derives from interference with English, the dominant language of the children who took part in the study. However, it is interesting to note that transfer effects have also been reported, albeit to a lesser extent, from the nondominant to the dominant language. For instance, in the case of English-German bilinguals, the transfer of German syntax can result in an ungrammatical utterance (12) rather than the grammatical target (13).

(12)   *I want look have.

(13)   I want to have a look.

Interference effects were also found between typologically distant languages. A study by Yip and Matthews (2007) found that one of the 2-year-old Cantonese-English bilinguals in the study produced interrogative sentences in English without interrogative phrase movement (14) and other sentences with object omission (15). Both cases exemplify interference effects from Cantonese, the child's dominant language, in which interrogative phrases are not moved and the omission of the object is allowed.

(14)   *It is for what? [Target: What is it for?]

(15)   *I don't want. [Target: I don't want it].

It is important to point out that these interference effects do not imply confusion for bilinguals, but merely reflect the natural path of acquiring grammatical properties in two languages. This developmental path, despite the initial interactions, will quickly reach the same level as that of monolinguals. It also seems that the interference effects are more marked from the dominant to the nondominant language, implicating an important relationship between language exposure and morphosyntactic development.

This is in line with what has been reported in monolingual studies that highlight a close relationship between development of lexical and grammatical skills. Having a richer lexicon in early developmental stages (e.g., between 18 and 30 months) indeed leads to faster and more accurate development than morphological and syntactic abilities (Dale et al., 2000). Research conducted by Marchman et al. (2004) suggests that this finding also applies to bilinguals. In the study, Marchman et al. analyzed the grammatical skills of English-Spanish bilinguals aged 17–30 months, the authors found that the breadth of the lexicon and the grammatical skills were strongly correlated in each of the languages. This implies that on the one hand, bilinguals will have more developed grammatical skills in the language in which they have the richest vocabulary, and on the other hand, that there is early linguistic differentiation in which both languages develop in a largely autonomous and independent manner.

Returning to the three hypotheses on the existence of two language systems in one mind (Figure 2.1), it therefore seems that the second one – which holds that the two language systems are autonomous, albeit not identical to monolinguals, but have the potential to interact – is the most accurate representation. Although the results from many studies are quite consistent in suggesting that the two language systems develop independently, this does not imply that there is not a certain degree of interaction between them. After all, as we will see in Chapter 4, they share neural substrates.

The acquisition of L2 morphosyntax in consecutive bilinguals deserves a separate discussion. It has been found that, especially in initial stages, bilinguals may be less accurate than monolinguals in understanding and especially in producing morphosyntactic complex sentences. For example, particularly difficult structures to acquire in Romance languages such as French and Italian are clitic object pronouns, such as le in the sentence in (16):

(16)   L'enfant   le mange.
         The child it eats.
         "The child eats it."

Clitic pronouns are monosyllabic and unstressed pronouns that cannot occur in isolation. They must always be accompanied by the verb, which makes them less phonologically salient. In Italian, on a morphological level, clitic objects are inflected for gender and number, giving rise to four distinct forms: *la, lo, le, li.* Syntactically, they precede the inflected verb, as shown in (as in "Il bambino la mangia", 'The child eats it')), but follow an infinitive (e.g., "il bambino vuole mangiarla" The child wants to eat it). Furthermore, the use of a clitic object is required only in specific pragmatic contexts, when the referent of the speech is unclear or has just been introduced. Consider, for example, the following exchanges in Italian (17) and Catalan (18):

(17)   a. Cosa fa   il   bambino con la mela?
            What is.doing the child   with the apple
            "What is the child doing with the apple?"
    b. La mangia.
         It   he eats
         "He eats it.3sg.fem."
    c. Mangia la mela.
         "He eats the apple."
    d. *Mangia.
         "He eats."

(18)   a. Què fa   el nen?
            What is.doing the child
            "What is the child doing?"
    b. La   veu.
         Her   he sees
         "He sees her."
    c. Veu   la   noia.
         "He sees the girl."

Only (17b) constitutes an appropriate answer to the question in (17a), in which the referent, the apple, has just been introduced into the speech. No native speaker would respond with (17c), which sounds inappropriate and redundant, or with (17d), which is ungrammatical. Conversely, (18b) cannot be used in response to (18a) in a context where the referent, the girl, has not yet been named, as it would be ambiguous. In this case, therefore, only (18c) is an appropriate answer.

The fact that the production of clitic pronouns involves different levels of complexity implies that it is a particularly difficult structure to acquire for monolinguals, who begin to produce them around 2 years of age. Before this point and even until around the age of 4, they omit them variably, pronouncing ungrammatical sentences as in (17d). This stage of clitic omission extends up to the age of 6 in monolingual children with Developmental Language Disorder (DLD). A study by Vender et al. (2016) found that the production of clitics was difficult even for 4- to 6-year-old Albanian-, Arabic-, and Romanian-Italian bilinguals who had been exposed to L2 Italian for about two years. The most frequent mistake the three groups of bilinguals made, unlike what is reported for monolinguals with DLD, was not clitic *omission*, but rather incorrect clitic *production*. Moreover, the error found in the majority of the incorrect utterances was related to grammatical gender (e.g., using the masculine pronoun *lo* instead of the feminine pronoun *la*). This suggests that, although the production of clitics is difficult for both monolinguals with DLD and bilinguals, it is still possible to identify distinct acquisitional characteristics based on the type of error committed. We will return to discuss this in more detail in Chapter 5.

It is also interesting to note that in the study by Vender et al. (2016), bilinguals' accuracy was significantly related both to their proficiency in the L2 Italian, measured by vocabulary and sentence comprehension tests, and to their amount of L2 exposure. In particular, bilinguals exposed to the L2 for the longest time not only had a richer vocabulary and a better understanding of clitics, but were also more accurate in producing them. This finding again points to the importance of the length of exposure to a language: if given the appropriate time to learn, bilingual children can acquire even the most complex structures to the same level as monolinguals. This was also demonstrated by a later study by Vender et al. (2018) who, by administering the same test to consecutive bilinguals exposed to L2 Italian for at least five years,

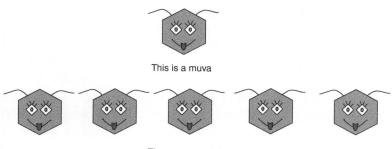

This is a muva

These are several...

Figure 2.3 Example of the nonword pluralization test. The Italian sentences used in the test were "Questa è una muva. Queste sono un po'di . . . (target: muve).

reported similar accuracy as monolingual peers. Finally, neither of these two studies reported L1-to-L2 transfer effects: all groups of bilinguals, in fact, committed the same type of error, regardless of how the L1 clitic pronominal system functions. This indicates that language exposure may be more relevant to acquiring complex structures than interlingual similarities and differences.

Despite these negative, albeit transitory, effects, it has been found that the knowledge of two language systems can lead to better morphological and metalinguistic skills in bilingual children. A study by Bialystok et al. (2014) showed that consecutive school-aged English-French bilinguals were more accurate than their monolingual English-speaking peers on the Wug Test (Berko, 1958), an inflectional morphology test in which children are asked to inflect nonwords (but phonologically plausible in the reference language) by forming the plural or the past participle. These results were also found in Albanian-Italian and Romanian-Italian bilinguals who were asked to produce the plural of invented words in Italian (Melloni et al., 2019). As illustrated in Figure 2.3, the children were shown an image and a sentence identifying what the image was, in this case an invented character called *muva*. Below, they were asked to complete another sentence which required them to pluralize the nonword. The results showed that the two groups of bilingual children performed similarly as – and, in some cases, even better than – their monolingual peers. As we will see in Chapter 5, a similar advantage was also reported by Vender et al. (2018a) in both typically developing bilingual children and those age-matched bilinguals with developmental dyslexia.

2.5   Bilingualism Does Not Create Confusion

Throughout this chapter we have discussed the acquisition of phonological, lexical, and morphosyntactic competence in bilingual children and have compared their typical development stages and times to that of monolingual children. We have seen that bilinguals are able to immediately differentiate the two language systems, leading to an important consideration: if the acquisition of language is already a notable achievement for a monolingual child, being able to master two of them simultaneously at the same level and rate is an amazing feat.

Parents and educators who are worried about creating confusion in babies who are immediately exposed to two languages should be reassured: the results of research conducted so far clearly and consistently indicate that simultaneous exposure to two languages does not create confusion for children whose brains appear to be predisposed to acquire a number of languages simultaneously, effortlessly, and without the need for explicit instruction. In fact, exposing babies immediately to more than one language familiarizes them with the two linguistic systems, including their phonological nuances that can be difficult to conquer in later age, without compensating their overall language development when compared to monolingual peers.

However, it is essential to remember that achieving optimal proficiency in both languages is only possible if there is a minimum of exposure to each language. Although in an ideal situation, a bilingual's input should be 50 percent in each of the two languages, this is not common. Nonetheless, it is recommended that exposure to each language be at least 30 percent. Below this threshold, exposure to the nondominant language risks being insufficient to ensure native competence in all linguistic domains. We will explore this topic further in Chapter 6.

Finally, it is important to remember that achieving a similar competence as age-matched monolinguals does not mean having identical performance across various linguistic domains. As we have seen, there can be significant differences, for example in lexical domain. However, we must also keep in mind that bilinguals are not the sum of two monolinguals, but instead, should be considered individuals who develop linguistic competence in two languages according to their specific needs and contexts. Any differences in language abilities between monolinguals and bilinguals, therefore, should not be cause for worry, but rather should be viewed as the natural development path that characterizes bilingualism.

Summary

In this chapter we have looked at linguistic aspects of the acquisition of two languages in bilingual children. We have observed that simultaneous bilinguals generally reach language milestones at the same age as monolinguals, showing no signs of confusion or delay. We have discussed how bilingual infants' phonological competence develops in both languages and learned that they display sensitivity to both sound systems even from the first days of life. As for lexical development, although monolinguals typically display a larger vocabulary than bilinguals, when considering both languages, bilinguals demonstrate a larger mental lexicon. Finally, we have considered the acquisition of morphosyntactic abilities in bilinguals and explored how they differ from those of monolinguals, while also discussing the role of language exposure on grammatical development and the possible advantages that bilinguals appear to have in tasks measuring morphological and metalinguistic skills.

Discussion Topics

1. Provide two or three examples suggesting that bilingualism does not cause confusion and that infants are able to separate the sounds in their two languages early on.
2. Referring to the Complementarity Principle, discuss how bilinguals' vocabulary is influenced by their linguistic needs.
3. Talk about the advantages that bilingualism can have on children's lexical development.
4. We mentioned that for bilingual children language milestones are acquired at the same times as for monolingual children. Discuss a few of these milestones.

5. Elaborate on the role of language exposure in the development of morphosyntactic skills in bilinguals.
6. In terms of grammar acquisition, talk about a few of the differences between simultaneous and consecutive bilinguals.
7. Provide and talk about an example of how bilingualism can provide advantages in morphological skills.

3 BILINGUALISM ACROSS THE LIFE SPAN

Chapter Objectives

- Explore the effects of bilingualism with an emphasis on cognition;
- Learn about different components of executive functions in the bilingual brain;
- Discuss bilingualism critically as a cognitive reserve; and
- Read about the benefits and challenges of learning a language as an adult.

3.1 Bilingualism and Cognition

For bilinguals, the brain has the ongoing commitment of simultaneously managing two or more language systems at rapid speed. In fact, the exercise of alternating between two languages, and selecting the appropriate one for a given communicative situation, not only has an effect on the development of the two languages themselves, but also on the brain itself, which can be measured over the course of life. From a series of studies conducted on different bilingual speakers, it appears that bilingualism promotes certain cognitive behaviors in the brain such as efficiently switching from one language to another and inhibiting the language that is not needed at that time (Baum & Titone, 2014). Moreover, some important cognitive differences between bilinguals and monolinguals have been reported in several studies. This debate is still ongoing and there are many complex variables that may play a role (Bialystok, 2009).

In the last twenty years, research on bilingualism has examined the hypothesis that knowing multiple languages modifies certain cognitive abilities including executive control, often referred to as executive functioning. What is meant by executive control and what aspects of it does bilingualism potentially modify? The research is still ongoing and there are many unclear answers, as we will see throughout this chapter. Generally, the reported differences in executive functions between bilinguals and monolinguals appear to persist over the course of life and are most pronounced when examining developmental trajectories among children or cognitive decline in aging populations (Bialystok, 2009). Furthermore, it has been observed that bilingualism could support cognitive reserve, the mind's resilience to effects of cognitive decline. It should be noted that the approach often used in these studies is to directly compare differences between monolinguals and bilinguals. However, this is not the most suitable way to examine these issues, since neither bilinguals nor monolinguals constitute homogeneous groups. It is plausible that individual differences in cognitive abilities or sociocultural factors shape the experience of each bilingual such that they impact the proposed link between language and cognition. For example, research that exclusively includes bilingual university students as participants, a population that often has socio-economic and cultural advantages, may not represent the entire bilingual population.

For monolinguals, there also is considerable variability, with some participants demonstrating distinct linguistic behavior compared to other monolinguals in the same language (Pakulak & Neville, 2010). These individual differences must also be considered when attempting to study the effects of two languages on cognition and/or the brain. In the case of older adults, the variability can be even more complex, given that other aging effects are brought into play, such as the decline of perceptual and sensory processing and motor responses. For bilinguals, there are substantial differences in the linguistic experiences involved in developing two languages. This is apparent when considering that a bilingual may have learned the two languages simultaneous from a very early age or much later in life – two very different linguistic situations.

As such, various degrees of linguistic competence can emerge depending on these bilingual experiences.

Among other things, the perception that society has toward bilingualism has changed in recent years with more adults now taking the advice of learning a language as adults with benefits beyond knowledge of two language systems.

Finally, when constructing research hypotheses, it is necessary to consider sociocultural characteristics that may be specific to a particular region or age group. For example, in a study by Garraffa et al. (2017) on Sardinian-Italian adult bilinguals who were residing in the city of Nuoro in Sardinia, linguistic profiles in Italian (the dominant language) and in some cognitive skills, such as working memory, were gathered, and compared to those of monolingual Italian speakers living in the same region but not using Sardinian (the regional language). The results showed that regardless of educational level, the most active bilinguals (i.e., those who made greater use of Sardinian) had higher working memory capacity than those who did not make extensive use of the language. This study, among others, suggests that bilingualism with a minority language may offer unique advantages given that minority languages often have no written counterpart. Consequently, bilinguals must perform language tasks – even as simple as remembering what foods to buy later at the store – without seeing it in written form. It is therefore important to consider environmental aspects of bilingualism, such as how often and with whom the two languages are used, in addition to the modality of such use, which, in the case of regional languages like Sardinian, is often only oral. An advantage over memorization due to the absence of writing was also referenced in Plato's *Phaedrus*. In one of the dialogues, Socrates converses with Theaetetus and proposes that writing is a tool for remembering things. But Theaetetus replied that the creation of writing would decrease people's memory capacity.

In this chapter we will discuss some recent studies that underscore the importance of language learning both for general cognition and for the development of a healthy brain that can better deal with aging and potentially help to offset degenerative diseases. We will start by looking at the cognitive effects of bilingualism while trying to understand what it means to have a bilingual brain outside the domain of language, and what changes can be brought about by the continuous exercise of multiple languages.

3.2 Bilingualism and Executive Functions

In everyday life, the brain makes continuous choices, selecting the word it deems correct to describe a given situation while suppressing information that is less relevant or conflicting with the task at hand. To make even the simplest of choices, the brain utilizes a system of processes called **executive functions**. Executive functions refer to a set of mental processes (e.g., planning, control, coordination, monitoring, and engaging other cognitive processes, etc.) that are responsible for the cognitive control of behavior. For example, in a language experiment in which an atypical situation must be described (e.g., a cat biting a dog), the more typical situation (i.e., a dog biting a cat) will likely interfere if automatic processes are not controlled. In the case of the unimodal bilingual, using one language implies that the other must be suppressed, and perhaps more so when the language not currently being used is the dominant one. Bilinguals must also rely on inhibitory control in contexts in which both languages are simultaneously activated but only one is needed. Moreover, in communicative situations, bilinguals must detect, if not already known or established, the language spoken by the interlocutor, and adapt their language choice accordingly.

In the bilingual brain, both languages are always active, even if only one is used at a certain time. The unused language must therefore be constantly inhibited, even if to different degrees in distinct contexts: a mental exercise which, as evidenced by multiple studies, seems to have cognitive consequences. One of the most studied effects of bilingualism is whether there is an advantage in suppressing irrelevant stimuli. Often this is measured by interference control tasks whose experimental designs include left- and right-hand button responses that are congruent or incongruent to the location of stimuli. When the stimulus and response button coincide, responses are typically faster and more accurate compared to when they are incongruent. For example, as shown in the variation of the **Simon task** (Simon & Rudell, 1967) in Figure 3.1, participants see figures individually on a computer screen and are asked to press a button with their left hand if they see a square and another

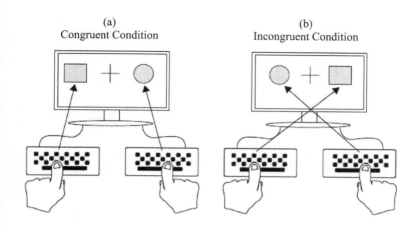

Figure 3.1 Experimental design used to measure the Simon effect.

button with their right hand if they see a circle. If the button response and location of the stimulus are congruent (Figure 3.1a), we should expect faster and more accurate responses due to the congruency between the stimulus and response. On the contrary, if the target shape appears on the opposite side of the screen as the button response (Figure 3.1b), we should expect slower and less accurate responses due to the need to inhibit the congruent response.

Simon tasks, like the version in Figure 3.1, require response control (i.e., suppressing the tendency to respond with the key that is congruent to the stimulus), inhibitory control (i.e., ignoring the position of the stimulus while focusing only on the shape), and working memory (i.e., keeping the two different sets of instructions in memory while performing a task). It has been hypothesized that bilinguals are more accustomed to inhibition tasks than monolinguals because the former continuously monitor diverse linguistic situations and inhibit the irrelevant language. Indeed, several studies have shown that bilinguals typically are less susceptible to the Simon effect and demonstrate faster processing speeds than monolinguals in congruent and incongruent conditions. These findings of better local inhibition of irrelevant information have often been used to support the argument for a **bilingual advantage**.

Another task that measures inhibition skills and that is often used with children is the **Opposite World task**, a verbal task in which

Figure 3.2 Example of the Opposite World task.

participants are asked to name numbers written on cards appearing in a single path. In the example in Figure 3.2, a participant is asked to read all the numbers (1 or 2) in the path from start to finish. Next, the participant is asked to repeat the task but respond with the opposite numbers (i.e., name "1" when seeing "2" and name "2" when seeing "1"). The difference in the naming time of the two tasks is used to index inhibition skills.

The opposite world task was used in another study comparing the performance of Sardinian-Italian bilingual primary school children to that of age-matched Italian monolinguals (Garraffa et al., 2015). The results showed better performance for bilingual children even though the test was administered in Italian and therefore, a disadvantage had been expected for the bilingual children. The findings also demonstrated that proficiency in Italian was similar for both bilingual and monolingual children, refuting the cliché that learning an L2 will somehow have negative consequences for proficiency in the majority language. On the contrary, the Sardinian-Italian bilingual children scored higher on Italian comprehension tests of sentences.

Another way in which the bilingual experience is distinct from that of the monolingual is related to their language choice in accordance with situational demands. It is not uncommon for bilinguals to use different languages for specific activities (e.g., German at work and Flemish at home and with family and friends). The cognitive system becomes used to preferring one language over another based on context and will keep the selected language active and readily accessible. This form of executive control is referred to as **global inhibition** and differs from local inhibition in that it is not responsible for domain- or task-specific operation within a language, but rather the entire language system. Many studies have reported the effects of global inhibition especially during production tasks which demonstrate the costs (in response times and accuracy) associated with switching between two languages, implicating a global selection system for language (Abutalebi et al., 2009). Therefore, the experience of the bilingual speaker differs from that of the monolingual in at least two factors: the bilingual experience requires the need to monitor activation within the two languages through executive control, and the need to exercise global control over the entire language system in order to select the correct language.

Another important point to emphasize is that the bilingual advantage appears to emerge in complex tasks that require concentration, overt responses, and cognitive effort. Conversely, in tasks that are automated and require fewer cognitive resources, there are generally little to no differences between monolinguals and bilinguals (Bialystok et al., 2005). In practice, to best test the differences between monolinguals and bilinguals, it is necessary to measure developmental trajectories and/or declines in executive functions. However, it is difficult to find differences in age when cognitive functions are considered stable values. Moreover, not all studies have reported effects of bilingualism on executive functions. Thus, the debate about whether and how bilingualism modifies the brain and cognitive abilities is still open and needs further research.

Bilingualism Matters

Bimodal Bilingualism and Its Effects on Cognition

An interesting population to consider in the research on the cognitive benefits of bilingualism are bimodal bilinguals, that is, hearing signers who can use both a spoken and a signed language. When a bimodal bilingual uses the two languages, suppression of one of the languages does not occur, or it occurs in a different way compared to bilingual speakers, as the two languages can be simultaneously activated and implemented via different output channels, namely verbal and gestural. On the contrary, signers of two sign languages should demonstrate similar cognitive benefits to those recorded for bilingual speakers of two spoken languages. There is not much research on bimodal bilinguals, but research on the neurobiology of sign language has confirmed that sign production is left-lateralized, and phonological encoding for signs involves the same brain areas as oral sounds. The main differences between bilinguals and bimodal bilinguals happens at the stage of articulation, where signs are shifted toward locations on the body with an interesting system of coordination spread across the two manual articulators. This line of thought holds that bimodal bilinguals can demonstrate successful cases of knowing more than one language, as the two systems will be less in competition and potentially generate less cross-language interference. Moreover, the core principles that define a language (a system of sounds with meanings) is present for both sign and verbal languages in the left hemisphere with similar neurobiological mechanisms.

3.3 The Adaptive Control Hypothesis in Bilinguals

The constant need to manage the selection, activation, and inhibition of two languages has led to the hypothesis that bilinguals may have more developed cognitive control than monolinguals. The model that elaborates a specific adaptive language control system for bilinguals was formulated by Abutalebi and Green (2013) and integrates the experience and circumstances of bilinguals' dynamic and various linguistic environments. For example, it could be reasonably assumed that a bilingual living in an environment which has equal use of both languages in various contexts may switch between the two languages more often, but may not need to apply much inhibition, because the two languages are always kept active and can be understood by most people. Conversely, an environment in which there is a dedicated language for specific contexts may entail fewer language changes and require more inhibitory control of the language not in use. The model therefore predicts that the experience of bilingualism can have an impact on executive functions, and that an environment with multilingual interlocutors in which there is the possibility of constantly exercising both languages can modulate executive control in ways that are different from a diglossic context.

There are several models that describe executive control. In some of these models, there is a distinction between proactive/global control and reactive/local control (Green's, 1998, inhibitory control model). Other models hold that linguistic production, like other non-linguistic actions, should be divided into schemas which are routine (i.e., automatic schemas that do not include control systems) and others which are not routine (Abutalebi & Green, 2008; Shallice & Burgess, 1996). According to this view, L1 production corresponds to a communicative routine, as it is a consolidated and automatic skill, while the L2 is nonroutine, since the use of the L2 requires more cognitive resources for processing, particularly at lower proficiency levels.

Furthermore, speech production requires two levels of inhibitory control. First, at the largest level of language, inhibitory control modulates the activation and inhibition of the two languages in a global manner. This happens, for example, when a bilingual communicates with a monolingual speaker and therefore, must suppress the language that the monolingual does not speak. Second, at the word level, inhibitory control regulates the activation and inhibition of specific words in each language, so that the correct word matching onto the target concept is accurately selected (Green, 1986, 1998).

Abutalebi and Green (2008) incorporate neurocognitive evidence on language production in bilinguals into their discussion and identify the brain networks that are recruited during adaptive control processes. In particular, the cortical areas of the prefrontal cortex, the inferior parietal area, and the anterior cingulate cortex appear to be largely implicated. Subcortical areas, such as the basal ganglia and the caudate nucleus, are also recruited to help modulate competition between the two languages. The areas of the prefrontal cortex and the anterior cingulate cortex are additionally involved in nonlinguistic tasks related to executive functions, demonstrating a common domain between language control and other cognitive functions (Braver, 2012). Generally, the prefrontal cortex is associated with executive control and the anterior cingulate cortex with error monitoring mechanisms that send signals to reactivate executive control and help reduce future errors.

The authors also note that neurocognitive evidence shows that there is a relationship between L2 proficiency and executive control. If L2 proficiency is low, it requires more control mechanisms localized in the prefrontal cortex, leading to a less automatic process. Conversely, if L2 proficiency is very high, production becomes more automatic and less dependent on inhibitory control. This greater automatization of the L2 can have effects on the L1 such that there is increased effort due to a weakening of the L1 word-to-concept association or more instructions from the L2 into L1 production. In practice, at very high proficiency levels in the L1, we often see evidence of L2 interference into the L1 due to the greater degree of L2 automatization of L2. This phenomenon that we also discussed in Chapter 1 is called transfer and has been extensively studied in the bilingual literature. This suggests that changes in the L1 do not necessarily involve the loss or erosion of grammar, but are selective and restricted to linguistic options governed by pragmatic or contextual conditions (Sorace, 2011). Changes in the L1 due to transfer effects provide further evidence that the two languages interact and are not independent.

To summarize, research is developing theoretical models that support the idea that the activation of more than one language in the brain implicates the involvement of executive control in a qualitatively different way than in monolinguals. The cognitive consequences of these differences in the bilingual brain develop over the course of life, as does the level of competence acquired in both languages. It is important to remember that such effects have not been reported in all studies on bilingualism and that there are also several studies that have found no differences between monolinguals and bilinguals in executive function tasks (Paap & Greenberg, 2013), most likely due to the numerous factors that characterize the bilingual experience, but which are usually not fully considered in the analyses.

3.4 Bilingualism and Cognitive Reserve

It has been proposed that the prolonged and consistent experience with bilingualism leads to a reorganization of neural networks, creating an effective support for executive control and generating lasting, positive consequences on the brain (Craig et al., 2010). This is observable, above all, during cognitive decline. **Cognitive decline** is the natural physiological process associated with aging in which certain cognitive abilities are slowed down and become less efficient. To help protect from this decline, it has been hypothesized that the brain can create a kind of **cognitive reserve** from activities that promote non-pathological aging. The concept of cognitive reserve (Stern, 2012) refers to the internal mechanisms that allow the brain to protect itself from disease and aging.

Much research has attempted to identify which specific factors from bilingualism and a bilingual lifestyle may have benefits. In addition to activities such as exercise, social interaction, and performing highly skilled tasks, bilingualism may foster cognitive reserve (Abutalebi et al., 2015; Bialystok et al., 2021). This arises from the constant use of multiple languages that has been shown to modify brain structures in a similar way to that which occurs in those with specialized skills, such as musicians (Bialystok & DePape, 2009). In testing the role of bilingualism in the development of degenerative diseases such as dementia, Bialystok et al. (2007) hypothesized that an increase in cognitive reserve among bilinguals may offset the first symptoms of cognitive degeneration. In the study, researchers conducted a retrospective analysis on patients who showed possible signs of dementia and were being treated at a memory clinic in Canada. Among the patients, bilinguals were identified who had used two languages for most of their life; the results demonstrated that bilinguals showed initial symptoms of dementia four years later than monolinguals, but no difference in the degree of degeneration following diagnosis. The findings suggested that bilingualism helps to delay the onset of cognitive decline but does not fundamentally modify the evolution of the brain's pathology. However, more recent studies suggest that once the initial symptoms appear, the disease may actually proceed *faster* in bilinguals than in monolinguals (Berkes & Bialystok, 2022). Clearly, more studies are needed to better understand the effects of bilingualism on onset and recovery patterns.

The study by Bialystok et al. (2007) was motivation for several subsequent investigations seeking to identify the various factors that may modulate the relationship between cognitive decline and bilingualism. In a study in India, Alladi et al. (2013) compared the age at which the first symptoms emerged among patients (391 bilinguals and 257 monolinguals) with various types of dementia (Alzheimer's, frontotemporal dementia, and vascular dementia). The researchers also examined whether the number of languages spoken, education level, profession, among other factors, had an effect. The results showed that the bilingual patients had a delay of about 4.5 years in the onset of first symptoms. This finding was not sensitive to years of formal education, speaking more than two languages, living in rural vs. urban areas, gender, or profession. The study was the first to consider both different types of dementia and different types of bilingualism, including factors such as the place of residence of the participants and their educational level, which in certain areas of India also includes people without education. Further studies are needed on other populations of bilinguals to better understand the effect of bilingualism on cognitive reserve. Crucially, as these studies position bilingualism in a positive light that fosters awareness of the benefits of bilingualism across the life span, policymakers should keep in mind the importance of their implications for both cognitive well-being and for health care costs.

3.5 Bilingualism for Healthy Aging

Cognitive aging can be depicted as a struggle between retaining the knowledge accumulated over the course of life and the natural decline of the cognitive abilities that support this knowledge and its processes. Older adults over 65 years of age typically have excellent vocabulary skills and advanced abilities in integrating contextual information during communicative acts. Although this is a result of extensive experience and knowledge (Wingfield & Tun, 2007), it is accompanied by a decline in sensory functions (hearing, sight) and executive functions (working memory, inhibitory control), due to natural physiological aging. Regarding the linguistic processes that rely on executive functions, such as resolving conflicts between competing elements during language production, older adults show slower response times in word selection tasks (Abada et al., 2008). Accordingly, an integrated vision has been put forth of how the constant linguistic exercise of bilingualism can somehow compensate for the cognitive decline of executive functions. As we discussed, bilinguals are engaged in constant monitoring that helps resolve conflicts between the two language systems (Abutalebi

& Green, 2008). In a longitudinal study (Bak et al., 2014) of 853 mono-lingual and bilingual participants, first tested at the age of 11 in 1947 and then retested between 2008 and 2010, bilinguals scored higher than their predicted scores from childhood compared to monolinguals. The largest differences between their actual scores and those they were predicted to have were on certain tasks such as general intelligence and reading skills. Moreover, these effects were found both among bilinguals who had grown up with two languages (i.e., they were bilin-gual in 1947) and individuals who learned it later in life (i.e., they were monolingual in 1947 but were bilingual by 2008). The study suggests that bilingualism may have positive effects on cognition among aging adults and that that these effects appear to apply to both early and late bilinguals.

The protective effect of bilingualism has been attributed to bilinguals' heightened use of inhibitory control required to navigate between various language contexts. In a longitudinal study by Kavé et al. (2008), the researchers tested a large sample of aging multilingual adults at three different stages over a twelve-year period. The findings revealed a significant correlation between the number of languages spoken and better performance on a variety of cognitive tasks, corro-borating the hypothesis that competence in more than one language has a beneficial effect on cognition. Another interesting question investi-gated is whether the cognitive advantage reported for bilinguals is evident, or even greater, in trilingual speakers. Although research in this area is still in its infancy, a study by Madrazo & Bernardo (2018) reported an advantage in inhibitory control in Chabacano-Filipino-English trilinguals compared to Filipino-English bilinguals.

Research has also reported that prolonged bilingualism, in addition to delaying the possible pathological effects of aging as dis-cussed above, can contribute to recovery from brain traumas, such as those arising from a stroke. In a study by Alladi et al. (2013) the profiles of 608 post-stroke patients were examined to investigate the role of bilingualism in predicting cognitive impairment after trauma in subjects who did not suffer from dementia. The survey results show that significantly more bilinguals than monolinguals maintain normal cognitive profiles (bilingual 40.5 percent, monolingual 19.6 percent). Furthermore, there is no difference in the onset of **aphasias** (the language disorder that is often acquired after brain trauma in the left hemisphere) between monolinguals and bilinguals, which means that bilingualism is not an additional factor of complexity that favors speech disorders in post-stroke subjects. Finally, subjects who developed vascular dementia or mild cognitive impairment were mostly monolinguals. The study, therefore, confirms the hypothesis that bilingualism can protect against stroke outcomes by significantly reducing the negative effects of cognitive impairment.

Bilingualism Matters

Bilingualism in the Stroke Unit: Language Awareness as a Tool for Health Equality

With most speakers in the world being bilingual, it is not uncommon to see cases of language disorders in bilingual patients caused, for example, by a stroke. The proposal that bilingualism can contribute to the brain's cognitive reserve by delaying mechanisms of neural degeneration has motivated researchers to address whether bilingualism can also be a protective factor against strokes and/or the severity of a stroke. Learning additional languages can be protective both before and after an acquired brain injury (Dekhtyar et al., 2020). These preliminary results are not suggesting that bilingual speakers are less likely to develop a neurological event that can cause aphasia. Indeed, multiple variables can factor into onset of a stroke. However, results do suggest that although bilingual speakers are at equal risk as monolinguals of developing aphasia after a stroke, their aphasia is likely to be less severe, a characteristic that has important implications on recovery patterns and quality of life after stroke (Paplikar et al., 2017).

Additional research on bilingual aphasia can also have an impact on speech and language therapy (SLT). Greater awareness about the properties of different languages can improve better rehabilitation protocols and intervention in language disorders (Crowley et al., 2015). Learning about (socio)linguistic issues during SLT training is rare in aphasia centres and in centres with a high number of patients from ethnic minorities, there are challenges among therapists whose language properties are very different from their patients (e.g., Charity Hudley et al., 2018). Unfortunately, the disparities in linguistic varieties may lead to misdiagnoses in patients who do not speak the same variety as those who are assessing their language disorder. To improve health service and reduce health inequality, more speech and language therapists are needed who can speak and use more than one language, better reflect their patient populations, and can apply sociolinguistic understanding of language variation in their assessment and intervention efforts.

3.6 Learning a Language as an Adult

So, is it worth learning a new language as an adult? Research on this question is ongoing, although there are indications that there is a cognitive benefit from language learning even for adults who have just started learning a new language. This may be especially the case after a short but intense learning period (Pot et al., 2018). For instance, Bak et al. (2016) compared a group of English-speaking adults who attended a one-week intensive language course in Gaelic, a minority language spoken in some areas of Scotland, a control group of adults enrolled in a different course with comparable duration and intensity but not involving language learning, and another control group consisting of age-matched monolinguals who followed their normal routines. Prior to the treatment period, no differences were found between the three groups in terms of their attention and task-switching abilities. However, at the end of the week, the group that attended the intensive language course performed significantly better than the other two groups on selective switching tasks. Nine months later, a subset of the participants who had attended the language course was tested again. The results showed that the positive effects of the language course persisted among participants who had maintained language practice for at least five hours per week. The results were inconsistent for participants who maintained four hours or less per week, with large individual differences showing that some participants returned to their initial performance while others slightly worsened. The study is interesting for two reasons: the first is the positive and prolonged effects on attentional skills that arise from a short but intense period of language learning; and the second is that the study involves a minority language, Gaelic. It should be noted that human cognition does not differentiate between global languages and minority languages, or between official languages and regional dialects. The cognitive effects that we have discussed in this chapter and the neurological effects that we will discuss in Chapter 4 apply in the case of all language systems.

In a literature review on the effects of bilingualism for healthy aging, it was reported that language learning can have benefits for our society and economy (Klimova, 2018). This is a new field of research, and in comparison with intervention studies focusing on physical activities or healthy eating habits, there is still not much evidence of the effect of language learning on the enhancement of cognitive functions among healthy aging adults. The need for more research requires cross-discipline collaboration to consider which specific aspects of language learning indeed have a positive effect on the aging process.

An important question that remains unanswered in the literature on aging and bilingualism is how to translate the findings into recommendations that can have implications for the public. While this has been explored for other domains dealing with experience-related changes due to aging, such as exercise or cognitive training, there is still no literature that has translated language learning as a factor into guidelines for healthy aging. For example, in the literature on the influence of exercise on nerve cells, it has been suggested that exercise not only has beneficial effects on the nervous and circulatory systems, but that it also induces the production of important chemicals in the brain and helps with brain tissue survival and repair (Voss et al., 2011). It is also important to clarify that these studies are examining various individual differences in cognitive abilities, that is, to better understand why certain individuals benefit more than others from a certain type of exercise and experience (Garrett et al., 2012). Reflection on individual differences is a fundamental factor, since it is quite clear that no individuals behave or perform in the same way to a given stimulation.

The saying "It's never too late to learn" is very applicable to language learning. To learn a new language after retirement should be encouraged alongside an active, healthy lifestyle. Moreover, the mantra that "the early bird gets the worm" may also be applicable, in that two or more languages can and should be introduced at the earliest possible age to promote better potential for brain neuroplasticity and cognitive reserve. In combining these two sayings, it may be most appropriate to say, "Earlier is better, but later is great, too." Based on the studies available, it is not yet possible to propose large-scale recommendations regarding the consequences of bilingualism. However, the increase in studies on these issues may soon help identify which aspects of language learning are crucial for cognitive reserve. As suggested regarding other positive factors for healthy aging, interdisciplinary studies that can be proposed in the future will be fruitful when examining the brain areas and neural mechanisms associated with bilingualism and whether and how they change.

Summary

The chapter has presented research on the effects of bilingualism on cognition in several bilingual populations, including trilingual speakers and bimodal bilinguals. The adaptive control model has been discussed, together with experiments on several aspects of executive functions in both children and adults. We also elaborated on language learning in adulthood, including some pioneering research on bilingualism as a protective tool for healthy aging and as a factor contributing to cognitive reserve. Bilingualism is now under investigation in many populations with language disorders and has been shown to impact on both the recovery of the patients' impairments and on rehabilitation programs that can be tailored to the linguistic needs of patients. More research on language as a positive factor across the life span is needed, as these studies have the potential to improve language training for speech and language therapists, have measurable outcomes in language therapy, and many other important implications.

Discussion Topics

1. Talk about some of the cognitive factors that a bilingual experience may affect.
2. Discuss evidence for and against the links between bilingualism and cognitive reserve.
3. Elaborate on what the adaptive control model proposes about the bilingual brain.

4. Comment on the impact of bilingualism on strokes and the evidence supporting it.
5. Discuss why it is worth learning a language as an adult.
6. Talk about some of the factors that you would need to consider when designing a language course for adults who want to develop a healthier brain.
7. Give a brief overview of the relationship between research on bilingual aphasia and on acquired language disorders.

4 TWO LANGUAGES IN ONE BRAIN

Chapter Objectives

- Review neurolinguistics studies on the bilingual brain;
- Introduce the neurobiology of language in the brain; and
- Discuss data on the bilingual brain across phonology, semantics, and syntax.

4.1 The Neurobiology of Bilingualism

In Chapter 2, we discussed the learning path that gives rise to bilingualism. Our linguistic competence, however, can also be investigated by examining its neurobiological characteristics through use of innovative and very sensitive neuroimaging methods. These measures allow us to capture the functional resolution of the brain and to study what happens to this important organ when processing linguistic stimuli (Del Maschio & Abutalebi, 2019).

It is important to keep in mind that becoming a speaker of two or more languages is a process in which environmental and biological factors play an important role. There is a biological predisposition to learn multiple languages, but you also need an ideal environment for this to happen. The path of this language learning process, and the degree of success or failure, are the basis for understanding the factors that condition the ability to acquire a language and, more generally, the ability to manipulate new symbolic systems. Studying bilingualism therefore proves to be a unique opportunity to examine the neurobiological bases of learning new information and the likely predisposition to learn multiple languages.

In this chapter we will focus on the effects of bilingualism on the brain and, in particular, in studies using electrophysiological and neuroimaging methods that seemingly suggest that bilingualism is capable of modifying the brain, both physiologically and cognitively, opening new horizons on the effects of bilingualism on human cognition and brain.

As new research on the bilingual brain is constantly being conducted, it is important to clarify that what we discuss in this chapter could easily be questioned by new studies or discoveries. This is a factor common to sciences that are based on modern techniques which, in turn, can undergo significant methodological and theoretical changes. We will start with a general reflection on some evidence regarding the bilingual brain, followed by the main themes related to the linguistic domains of phonology, syntax, and semantics.

A study by Swedish researchers reported that learning a language, even in adulthood, can have observable effects on the brain (Mårtensson et al., 2012). The study compared a group of young adults (i.e., at the peak of their cognitive abilities) immediately after attending intensive language courses in either Arabic, Persian, or Russian, and a control group of age-matched students who were also enrolled in intensive courses, but of another kind (classroom lessons of different subjects). Comparison of brain images measured with **magnetic resonance imaging (MRI)** showed that specific areas of the cerebral cortex, particularly the superior temporal gyrus and hippocampus, had developed in the intensive language learners, but not in the control group. Furthermore, the effects were greater for those who had achieved higher linguistic proficiency and accuracy in the L2.

The fact that there is an interaction between the development of specific brain areas and learning an L2 is promising. A synthesis by Stein et al. (2014) found consistent findings showing cortical gray matter modifications such that there were structural changes in the left inferior frontal and inferior parietal regions, and in studies on white matter connectivity, there are changes to the anterior parts of the corpus callosum. Similar findings have been reported in a study including over 1,300 bilinguals by Pliatsikas et al. (2020). In comparing monolingual and bilingual brains across the life span, the authors reported:

> Bilingual and monolingual participants manifested distinct developmental trajectories in both grey and white matter structures. As compared to monolinguals, bilinguals showed: (a) more grey matter (less developmental loss) starting during late childhood and adolescence, mainly in frontal and parietal regions (particularly in the inferior frontal gyrus pars opercularis, superior frontal cortex, inferior and superior parietal cortex, and precuneus); and (b) higher white matter integrity (greater developmental increase) starting during mid-late adolescence, specifically in striatal–inferior frontal fibers. (p. 2131)

A study by Voits et al. (2022) found that greater hippocampal volume correlated with quantified dual language use, suggesting that long-term bilingualism may be related to neuroprotective effects in the hippocampus. In a longitudinal study by Liu et al. (2022), the researchers examined the effects of L2 learning on grey matter structure and found that structural adaptations occurred in the left anterior cingulate cortex and right inferior frontal gyrus after L2 learning for one year. Critically, these modifications correlated with changes in the learners' cognitive control across the learning. For reviews on the neuroanatomical consequences and pathological implications of bilingualism, see DeLuca et al. (2020) and Taylor et al. (2022).

Neuroimaging can also be used in studies whose objective is to explore language functioning, such as which parts of the brain are activated during various linguistic tasks. To do this, it is necessary to use experimental paradigms that isolate a specific language component to test, such as the discrimination of sounds for phonological competence or word naming for lexical access. However, many operations we do with language interact with each other, and it is difficult to truly separate linguistic functions. Nonetheless, some studies have made use of **artificial languages** with the aim of isolating a particular linguistic phenomenon. An artificial language is an invented linguistic system, obviously more restricted than a natural language, with a series of elements and rules that can be inferred implicitly or explicitly simply through exposure to the artificial language.

In an artificial language study by Morgan-Short et al. (2015), a group of adults was explicitly taught a language rule, similar to formal L2 courses in which the teacher explains a grammar rule (e.g., the auxiliary "do" must be added in negative sentences in English). A second group was exposed to this language rule implicitly in an immersion setting. In both explicit and implicit learning groups, there were observable effects on the brain. However, the participants who had been implicitly exposed to the rule in the artificial language showed neurophysiological mechanisms similar to native speakers of natural languages. Furthermore, when tested again after six months, these participants' brains maintained these effects even though they had not further exposure to the artificial language after the initial testing.

Other studies have shown that individuals who show a special talent for recognizing sequences and patterns, as is needed in artificial language learning tasks, more effectively learn the grammar of the artificial language under immersion situations, demonstrating that even as adults, if exposed to a consistent and optimal stimulus, it is possible to learn a language, but that some cognitive skills of implicit learning are necessary and may even be at the root of individual differences in L2 learning (Morgan-Short, 2014). The future of neuroimaging studies will provide us with interesting insights about the skills involved in learning new stimuli. It will be important to verify whether cognitive abilities have significant implications for L2 learning and to correlate certain learning abilities to their optimal learning environment or instructional method, including explicit instruction that offers direct presentation of grammatical rules, implicit learning such as immersion settings that foster inference of a rule without explicit instruction or, even better, a combination of the two.

In Chapter 3, we discussed bilingualism and the brain, including the potential cognitive advantages of learning more than one language. We also reviewed pioneering studies on the possible relationship between brain degeneration in dementia and its relationship with bilingualism. These preventive effects on the decline of cognitive and biological functions can be observed throughout the lifespan and it is not necessary to be a highly proficient bilingual for these effects to emerge. In this chapter, we will focus on the neurobiological aspects of bilingualism that are related to language in the strict sense. As we will see, the two themes of Chapters 3 and 4, namely the cognitive profiles at the level of executive functions and neurobiological modifications in the bilingual brain, respectively, are interconnected because it is precisely the biological modifications that protect the cognitive mechanisms of brain functioning, even if we still do not know exactly which ones are at work, how, and to what degree.

Bilingualism Matters

The Neuroplasticity of the Bilingual Brain

Our brain is continuously shaped and sculpted by our actions and experiences. This phenomenon is a crucial ability in the recovery from brain disfunctions, as well as for supporting activities that facilitate the healthy development of the brain. Neuroplasticity refers to the brain's malleability, that is, its ability to be easily influenced, trained, or controlled by external events. Neuroplasticity occurs throughout the lifespan and involves the reorganization of brain cells. It can occur because of learning, experience, and memory formations, or because of damage to the brain.

While people used to believe that the brain became unmodifiable after a certain age, recent research has revealed that the brain never stops changing in response to learning. There are things that can encourage your brain to adapt and change. To improve neuroplasticity, for example, you can enrich your environment, living in a learning environment that offers opportunities for novelty, focused attention, and engagement in challenging activities (Vemuri et al., 2014).

It has now been argued that language learning is among the activities that can support neuroplasticity of the brain. Together with well-known healthy habits, such as dieting, exercising, or playing an instrument, to learn a foreign language should be one of the recommended activities that supports healthy aging and reinforces the brain structure. While research on language learning as a tool to support brain neuroplasticity is still in its infancy, it is possible that more studies can eventually inform ways of creating personalized plans to support a healthy brain.

4.2 The Organization of Languages in the Brain

Let's start our discussion about language in the brain with purely linguistic factors. Throughout its development, the brain is stimulated by several linguistic codes, for example by input from caregivers of a child who speak two different languages. First, we must ask ourselves if the brain considers these codes distinctively or whether the input of both languages passes through a single **linguistic processor**, a network of neural areas that are responsible for coding what we want to express and decoding what we hear. The question of whether or not the two linguistic systems are separated has also been addressed by neuroimaging studies. These studies have shown how often both languages are analyzed by a single linguistic processor, regardless of linguistic modality (i.e., comprehension or production). A critical factor in these studies is not the age at which an individual was first exposed to the languages, but rather the amount and quality of exposure to the two languages.

Before venturing into bilingual brain research, it is necessary to present a language model that unifies the evidence gathered on language processing in the brain. One of the most well-cited models, which integrates both the various linguistic modules and the different linguistic modalities, is the dual-stream model of speech processing (Hickok & Poeppel, 2007). A simplified version of the model is shown in Figure 4.1.

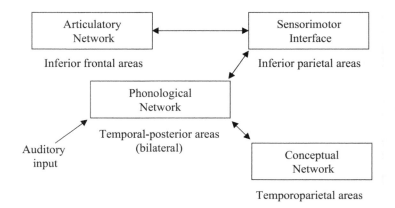

Figure 4.1 Dual-stream model of speech processing and cortical areas for language.

According to the dual-stream model, linguistic input is analyzed by two processes that flow through dorsal and ventral paths. The dorsal path leads to the parietal lobe, which is involved with processing spatial information and the ventral stream leads to the temporal lobe, which is responsible for identification and recognition. This highly lateralized **dorsal pathway** in the left hemisphere, otherwise known as the "where" pathway, integrates the auditory and motor systems. In practice, the dorsal pathway encodes sounds and converts them into motor articulatory planes for decoding. Let's walk through an example of linguistic input flowing through the dorsal path. First, the auditory information that we perceive through the auditory canal is processed by the superior temporal gyrus. From here it begins its journey in the dorsal way, where it is transmitted to the left sylvian parietal-temporal areas. Finally, the information passes to the articulatory system, which corresponds to motor movements that are specialized for language production. It is interesting to note that the dorsal path proposed in the dual-stream model is a supramodal path, that is, an interface between the sensory and motor systems. This may explain why languages that use communication modalities based on nonauditory sensory domains, such as sign language, are processed in a very similar way to spoken languages.

Within the dorsal network, the frontotemporal regions (i.e., the frontal and temporal lobes of the brain) are connected by the arcuate fasciculus, which is characterized by a strong anatomical asymmetry so that the long direct segment of the arcuate fasciculus has greater volume in the left hemisphere compared to the right. This has been further verified in studies using **Diffusion Tensor Imaging** (DTI), a neuroimaging technique in which the main white matter fiber bundles are visualized three-dimensionally (Catani & Mesulam, 2008). This technique therefore allows the mapping of connections between the primary brain areas involved in a given process and has shown that the two fundamental centers for language (Broca's and Wernicke's areas) are connected in a nonmediated way through the arcuate fasciculus? and that this direct connection occurs only in the left hemisphere (Catani et al., 2007).

The model also makes precise predictions about language disorders in which damage to the dorsal pathway leads to disconnection conditions such as **conduction aphasia**. In conduction aphasia, characterized by a difficulty in repeating words but intact auditory understanding of language, individuals perfectly understand what they hear but cannot reproduce the linguistic message.

The ventral path, otherwise known as the "what" pathway, has an important role for language as it characterizes incoming stimuli as linguistic and gives it a specific meaning. In neuroanatomical terms, the ventral pathway is activated when linguistic information passes through the middle posterior temporal gyrus: in this phase, individual sounds are transformed into linguistic symbols with significance values.

Against this backdrop of the dual-path model for language processing in the brain, we can pose research questions with clear hypotheses about what mechanisms are in place during specific linguistic tasks. We can also ask questions about the bilingual brain to better understand how we use these two paths and how we process linguistic elements from both languages in the brain. We will start with sounds, which are often one of the distinctive markers of a language. Each language selects a specific set of sounds that humans can perceive and produce and then builds words based on these sounds. Of course, not all languages include the same set of sounds: there are languages that have sounds that other languages simply do not have, which often causes phonological difficulties for speakers who have learned an L2 as teenagers or adults, as we saw in Chapter 2 (see Grimaldi, 2019).

4.3 Phonology in the Bilingual Brain

The phonological system, which underlies the ability to use the sounds of a given language and recognize them in a distinctive way, is one of the most complex systems to acquire for a L2 learners. Think of the dual-path model we have just described. Learning new sounds not only means decoding them (i.e., acoustically recognizing and discriminating them from possible competitors) but also learning new articulations that are required to reproduce them accurately. Given the speed of speech production (i.e., in typical conversation, humans produce on average between 130 and 140 words, or around 700 articulations of sounds, per minute) and the fact that linguistic systems make use of sounds that are not present in all languages, it is clear why learning and using the sounds of an L2 is not an easy task. All of us can recognize speakers who have a non-native accent when speaking in their L2 and often, we are even able to guess what their L1 is, based on their sound formations in the L2. Learning new sounds is a very difficult task, especially as it highly interferes with the sounds we have learned and are currently using in the L1.

There is evidence that prenatal bilingual exposure to two languages affects newborn babies' sensitivity to those two languages (Byers-Heinlein et al., 2010). Furthermore, it has been found that during the first year of life, we develop a type of perceptive attention specifically for the sounds that distinguish the language we are learning. Of all the possible learning options, the brain seems to economize and select only those relating to the language to which it is exposed. This selection ability is not present in newborns, who appear to be born with a universal repertoire of sound possibilities available that has not been selected as the language present in their environment. After the first year of life, the brain adapts to the environment and the perceptual sensitivity to non-native sounds gradually decreases (Kuhl et al., 2006; Werker & Tees, 2005). This cerebral reorganization serves to tune the dorsal pathway to certain perceptual categories, memorize them in long-term memory, and form the articulatory planes to produce them. The supramodal dorsal path then begins a feed-forward learning path; that is, a process of adaptation by trial and error that makes use of the feedback we have from our own auditory system when we listen to ourselves and that will take us from articulatory gestures to mental representations of sounds (Grimaldi, 2017). By around 2 or 3 years of age, when the output produced by the articulatory planes learned by the brain is compatible with the sound representations we have learned to decode, we are able to accurately articulate sounds in the language. Consequently, the brain becomes irrepressibly sensitive to language, in the sense that we cannot ignore linguistic stimuli that surround us. What we have just described is the biological process of the development of an L1 phonological system, which occurs naturally if a child is exposed to coherent linguistic input (i.e., a language spoken by a community of speakers).

What happens when an adult learns an L2? In the last twenty years, much progress has been made in research examining sound discrimination using **electroencephalography (EEG)**, a neurophysiological technique that measures and records the electrical activity produced by the brain. In this methodology, when an anomalous stimulus that deviates from the correct one is processed, an observable effect called an **event-related potential (ERP)** can be analyzed. ERP studies have made it possible to examine the L2 phonetic-phonological acquisition processes.

Many studies have compared immersion learning to formal learning contexts. Regarding the immersion context, one study showed that Hungarian speakers living in Finland discriminated phonemes in Finnish that did not exist in their L1 to the same degree as monolingual Finnish speakers (Winkler et al., 1999). These findings, however, appear to be distinct for formal learning contexts in that they may not lead to the formation of mnemonic traces of non-native sounds, even if it involves perceptual modifications that assist the discrimination and recognition of some sounds (Dobel et al., 2009). So, it appears that the learning of L2 phonological structures is favored in immersion situations, while formal classroom contexts may not create new learning paths in the auditory cortex.

Other research has investigated L2 phonological awareness by using neuroimaging techniques during repetition tasks (Ghazi-Saidi & Ansaldo, 2017), category identification (Conant et al., 2013), or passively listening to organized sequences of sounds from an artificial language (Maggu et al., 2019). One of the goals of these studies is to understand if the new sounds that are being learned in a new language are processed by the same brain regions as the L1 or whether they make use of other neural circuits. The phonological system in monolingual speakers has a precise neural substrate, as we saw in the dual-path model (see Figure 4.1). After incoming sounds have been determined to be linguistic stimuli, this sound input crosses a precise path that starts from the receptive system of the associative areas in the Perisylvian region and then passes through a large bundle of nerve fibers called the arcuate fasciculus that connects the Broca's and Wernicke's areas. Recent studies suggest that the first phase of this process has bilateral neural bases and, subsequently, with some exceptions, it relies on the left hemisphere by also making use of the working memory system found in the auditory–motor integrative circuit. A path in the dorsal areas projects the analyzed auditory stimulus from the posterior temporal areas to the areas of the premotor cortex, mediating between the phonological representation of sound and its articulatory representation.

A series of studies on the various language modules seems to indicate that bilinguals use the same path in both languages, making use of the dorsal path for auditory–motor interface and for the processing of new or complex sounds. We will see that this argument also holds true for other language modules such as syntax and semantics, both for individual words and sequences of words.

In a longitudinal study of L2 sound learning conducted with **functional magnetic resonance imaging (fMRI)**, minimal pairs of non-native sounds were presented, for example the /r/ - /l/ contrast for native Japanese adults (Callan et al., 2004). The participants, who had studied L2 English for around six years and were considered highly proficient, were explicitly trained to perceive the difference between similar sounds. This phonological discrimination training led to brain changes in bilingual speakers compared to monolinguals. In particular, an increase in activation was found in specific brain regions, including the superior temporal gyrus in both hemispheres, the premotor cortex, and subcortical regions. Callan et al. (2004) proposed that phonological discrimination is associated with greater and less selective brain activation, which demonstrates not only the perception of the phonological contrast, but also a coupling of the auditory–motor planes. This indicates that targeted training can induce changes in neural organization even in auditory areas and highlights the brain's capacity for reconfiguring itself, as a sort of acoustic plasticity, even for areas that are not subject to changes over the course of life.

In conclusion, for both L1 and L2 acquisition, several neuroimaging studies report an involvement of the areas dedicated to phonological processing, which is apparent through a dorsal audio–motor interface.

4.4   Morphology and Syntax in the Bilingual Brain

Grammatical competence is based on the ability to create and understand grammatical structures of a language. For instance, it is clear to English speakers that sentence (1) is incorrect even if its meaning is still understood. Where is the anomaly? Certainly, the sentence shown in (2) is preferred to (1), even though all of the words are the same. It is clear, then, that we are sensitive not only to accurate pronunciation of sounds but also to the order in which words are organized in sentences. We know that there are languages, such as English, in which adjectives precede nouns as in (2) and when nouns precede the adjectives as in (1), the result is ungrammatical. Other languages such as Arabic, Hebrew, Romanian (3), Vietnamese, and many others permit nouns to precede adjectives. Learning a grammar therefore means extracting and making use of the properties with which individual words are organized. Bilingual speakers can be influenced by the syntactic structure of a language, especially at early proficiency levels, and they can transfer some grammatical rules, such as the order of nouns and adjectives from one language to another. It should be noted, however, that these cross-linguistic effects are often short-lived as they are largely related to proficiency/competence and that bilinguals are often aware of the subtle differences between different linguistic systems.

(1)   * The bag green is on the table.

(2)   The green bag is on the table.

(3)   Geanta   verde   este pe   masă.
         The bag   green   is   on   the table.
         "The green bag is on the table."

Grammatical competence, that is, the ability to recognize and formulate well-organized sentences, can be studied through morphology or syntax. Morphology allows us to create complex words formed by roots and suffixes of various kinds (cf. Semenza et al., 2019). Morphological competence also involves phonological variables, and therefore, a certain difficulty is expected in bilingual speakers learning the new set of elements that must be added to words, such as grammatical gender marked in nouns or inflectional morphemes that are added to verbs.

In the neurolinguistic literature on morphological processing in monolinguals, the lower frontal gyrus in the left hemisphere is often referred to as the area involved in breaking down a word into its fundamental building blocks. There are numerous differences in the areas of activation both in relation to languages and the type of morphological operation required (e.g., inflectional processes such as adding -ed to a verb in English to create the past tense, or derivational processes such as adding the suffix-ness to an adjective such as "happy" to create the noun "happiness").

In an fMRI study, there were no differences on recognition task of regular verb forms between highly proficient bilinguals, who learned their L2 later in life, and monolinguals (Pliatsikas et al., 2014a). Both groups recruited similar language areas for regular versus irregular verbs, the latter of which are most likely processed as whole words and are not morphologically decomposed. It is possible to assume that word decomposition processes are the same for L1 and L2 regardless of age of acquisition.

Other neuroimaging studies have highlighted the existence of a unique mechanism shared by monolinguals and bilinguals. For example, a comparison of L1 Japanese speakers' brain images before and after learning verbal conjugations of the simple past in English showed that the same areas are activated for both L1 and L2 (Sakai et al., 2004). Moreover, the higher the participant's linguistic competence, the more the activations were similar to those of monolinguals. In addition to the fact that morphological processing is performed in a similar way in both languages from a neurological point of view, an increase in the volume of gray matter has also been reported for late bilinguals who have achieved high proficiency levels (Pliatsikas et al., 2014b).

Let's now turn to the purely syntactic ability of formulating and understanding word organization within sentences (Moro, 2016). In monolinguals, the brain network for syntactic involves Broca's area, the superior temporal gyrus, the basal ganglia, and the cerebellum (Cappa, 2012). Typically, neuroimaging studies demonstrate similarities between L1 and L2 with respect to frontotemporal network recruitment, with activations modulated by the learner's linguistic competence and the task's syntactic complexity (Wartenburger et al., 2003). These studies make use of **grammaticality judgment tasks** in which bilinguals are explicitly asked to judge the correctness of sentences of varying complexity in both languages (Bard et al., 1996; Sorace, 2010). Notably, there are no differences in accuracy or brain activation between L1 and L2 for both early and late bilinguals with high proficiency in both languages. However, late bilinguals with weaker L2 skills showed much more extensive brain activations, indicating less specific and less efficient linguistic processing (Golestani et al., 2007).

Bilingualism Matters

Neurological Damage and Aphasia in the Bilingual Brain

Aphasia is a chronic language disorder that affects speakers usually after neurological trauma, such as a stroke or head injury due to an accident. Aphasia is not a rare condition and today the issue of how to assess and treat bilingual patients with acquired language disorders is becoming more prominent in society and health care systems. There are several issues that are still unclear in bilingual aphasia. First, it is not fully understood why both languages are sometimes affected equally and other times unequally, and which language(s) should be selected for the treatment plan. The general consensus is that both languages should be assessed and that treatment should be conducted in the most preserved language. This approach implies a more person-centered care system in health services that is ready to quickly react to the specific type of impairment in bilingual speakers.

A second question is about the effect of having aphasia in a bilingual brain. It has been demonstrated that bilingualism is not a pejorative factor in aphasia: bilinguals who are diagnosed with aphasia do not suffer more extensive language disorders. On the contrary, some preliminary results suggest that bilingualism offers a positive effect on treatment of aphasia (Alladi et al., 2015). This suggests that bilingualism may play a role in preventing more severe language disorders, such as a global aphasia. Given that bilingual aphasics have access to more metalinguistic knowledge compared to monolingual aphasics, they may also develop more explicit adaptation to language disorders for which they are able to compensate. Bilingual aphasiology is a relatively new area within neurology and neurolinguistics and poses exciting opportunities for developing ameliorative treatments in language therapy and new horizons for discussing the benefits of the bilingual brain.

4.5   Semantics in the Bilingual Brain

Semantic competence concerns the ability to extract meaning from linguistic input. Many studies conducted on monolingual speakers have shown that meaning is developed in the brain by recruiting an extensive network of neural areas that appear to be conditioned by the

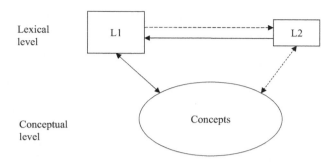

Figure 4.2 Revised Hierarchical Model (Kroll & Stewart, 1994).

experimental task and the type of input. We know from the dual-path model that semantics are processed via the ventral path (Hickok & Poeppel, 2000; Saur et al., 2008). However, the semantic-lexical domain is not as clear-cut: different brain regions appear to be involved in semantic tasks, including the anterior temporal lobes, the left fronto-temporal gyrus, and the posterior temporal areas (Cappa, 2012). Furthermore, at the subcortical level, the thalamus appears to be involved in tasks that require meaning extraction and new word learning (Del Maschio & Abutalebi, 2019).

An interesting research question with respect to the bilingual brain and semantics concerns the possibility that the new words learned in an L2 are mapped onto concepts that were originally formed in the L1. As shown in Figure 4.2, the **Revised Hierarchical Model** proposed by Kroll and Stewart (1994) argues that an abstract declarative memory exists, which consists of a common conceptual storage shared by both languages and a lexical memory that is separate for words in each language. According to the model, during the initial stages of L2 learning, new words must rely extensively on their L1 translation equivalent to access the concept onto which they are mapped. As the learner becomes more proficient in the L2, there is less dependence on L1 words, given that L2 words establish strong enough links with their conceptual representation.

In practice, L1 vocabulary is conceptually mediated, while initially, new L2 words learned must pass through their associated L1 translation to access the concepts. An interesting implication of the hierarchical model seems to be the close relationship between lexical competence and linguistic competence in which L2 age of acquisition is not a modulating variable (Green, 2003).

In many neuroimaging experiments that make use of various lexical tasks, such as the **verbal fluency task**, in which participants must spontaneously name words belonging to specified categories, the word repetition task, or tasks in which shapes are named, it is clear that the L2 competence contributes more than age of acquisition to the observed overlap of brain areas in the two languages (Illes et al., 1999).

Many studies on L2 word learning and syntax have shown that the reorganization of language in the brain begins very quickly at the earliest stages of learning in educational contexts. For example, a longitudinal ERP study measured sensitivity to recognizing words versus nonwords during a lexical decision task among monolingual English speakers who were enrolled in a four-month L2 Spanish course (Soskey et al., 2016). The participants were tested on three occasions and the findings revealed neurobiological changes related to the amount of L2 exposure. Specifically, the **N400 component**, the electrophysiological potential that occurs around 400 ms after exposure to a lexical violation, was modulated by the amount of exposure to the L2. Notably, participants with less exposure exhibited a large N400 component. This shows that the brain is able to very quickly integrate new words from another language into its lexical store, even if the language is learned as adults. Humans are always ready to learn new words: It is simply a matter of facilitating such learning with integration mechanisms and ensure that the processing stabilizes, as is the case with L1 word learning.

An interesting neuroimaging study was conducted on bilingual Friulian-Italian speakers, some of whom were simultaneous bilinguals (i.e., exposed to both languages from birth) and some were exposed to Friulian from birth and to Italian anywhere between ages 3 and 6 (Consonni et al., 2013). Participants from both groups were highly proficient in both languages but had more exposure to Italian, their dominant language. They were asked to carry out production and comprehension tasks in both languages. The results showed an overlap of the areas activated by the two groups during tasks in both production and comprehension. Moreover, in the Friulian tasks, the results showed more involvement of the left thalamus, a region associated with cognitive control. These findings may implicate a relationship between less exposure to a language and the cognitive control mechanisms that support it, due to the additional brain activity needed to maintain the activation of the nondominant language and to suppress the dominant language.

Although it seems that neurological activation is similar for bilinguals' two languages, the exact nature of the semantic-lexical task being used must also be taken into consideration. A study on late bilinguals revealed that verbal fluency tasks require the involvement of frontotemporal areas in bilinguals (Vingerhoets et al., 2003) but not in monolinguals. An increase in the volume of gray matter in bilinguals in the areas that change with vocabulary increases across the lifespan was found in tests on lexical competence (Richardson et al., 2010).

In conclusion, even for semantic-lexical functions, it seems that there is no significant neural distinction between bilingual and monolingual brain, apart from greater involvement of the anterior frontal cortex in bilinguals if their relative level of competence or amount of exposure to the language is inadequate or inconsistent. Moreover, the age of acquisition does not seem to have an effect when bilinguals have a high level of competence in the two languages.

Summary

Presenting evidence from studies that have adopted neuroscientific methods, this chapter has discussed the effects of bilingualism at the physiological level of language processing in the brain. In the first part, the dual-stream model was illustrated and concepts such as the neuroplasticity of the bilingual brain were discussed. The second part of the chapter presented more detailed illustrations of the effects of bilingualism in the brain across the linguistic domains of phonology, morphology, syntax, and semantics. The research in these areas is developing rapidly, and it is recommended that readers constantly review the literature.

Discussion Topics

1. What is the meaning of neuroplasticity? Discuss neuroplasticity with respect to the bilingual brain.

2. Describe the dual-stream model and its components. Try to come up with examples from different languages.
3. Discuss some studies that have specifically investigated phonology, morphology/syntax, and semantics in the bilingual brain.
4. Describe what the Revised Hierarchical Model hypothesizes. Then, illustrate your description through an example.
5. Discuss the evidence from the literature that discusses whether the brain distinguishes between minority languages and majority languages.
6. Describe what bilingual aphasia is and the social implications it has for society.
7. Which factors seem to "change" the bilingual brain? Discuss some evidence from neurolinguistics studies.

5 BILINGUALISM AND ATYPICAL DEVELOPMENT

Chapter Objectives

- Analyze patterns of language acquisition of bilingual children with atypical development;
- Explore the interaction between bilingualism and language disorders;
- Discuss advantages and disadvantages of bilingualism in children with atypical development; and
- Provide indications and suggestions for supporting bilingualism in children with atypical development.

5.1 Bilingualism and Atypical Development

Although, a few decades ago, it was believed that bilingualism could cause cognitive or linguistic delays, today, ongoing research has painted a very different scenario – one which highlights various cognitive, linguistic, and sociocultural benefits associated with the use of multiple languages. Thanks to the dissemination of these results, the importance of promoting and supporting bilingualism is now more explicit and it is becoming common practice to encourage children and adults alike to learn another language.

However, in cases of atypical development, in which an individual presents a specific disorder, especially in the language domain, the situation is more complex. These disorders can be broadly divided into two categories, based on their genetic nature and on their period of onset: **developmental disorders** are those in which the disorder is present from birth, and **acquired disorders** are those seen in individuals whose typical development is affected and/or deteriorates following brain trauma or damage. Among the developmental disorders, we find developmental dyslexia, autism, schizophrenia, intellectual disability, and Down syndrome. The most common acquired disorder is aphasia, which typically affects adults following vascular diseases such as a stroke, but which can also occur in children, following brain injuries or tumors.

In the presence of these types of disorders, unfortunately we tend to see bilingualism in a different light: many fear, in fact, that exposure to more than one language may cause further difficulties and slow down or even hinder linguistic and cognitive development. In reality, these are erroneous prejudices, not too different from those sometimes applied to typical bilingualism, seeing it as a cause of possible disadvantages until empirical-based studies that we mentioned in Chapter 3 proved otherwise.

Although scientific research on bilingualism in atypical development is relatively recent, studies quite unanimously show that exposure to two or more languages does not cause additional challenges in children and adults with language and cognitive disorders. As we will see, the linguistic difficulties of monolinguals and bilinguals affected by these types of disorders are typically the same, and in neither case do we see negative effects due to the presence of one or two language systems. On the contrary, some recent studies have highlighted how the cognitive advantages typically associated with bilingualism can also extend to those with atypical development, and potentially to a greater extent.

In this chapter we will focus on the relationship between bilingualism and Developmental Language Disorder (DLD), developmental dyslexia, autism, Down syndrome, and aphasia. We place particular emphasis on DLD and dyslexia, which are undoubtedly the most common, and on problems related to inaccurate diagnosis of these disorders among bilingual children. It often happens, in fact, that bilinguals, especially at early L2 proficiency levels, have a performance similar to that of monolinguals with DLD or dyslexia in certain linguistic areas such as reading and writing. The incidence of these disorders can therefore be both underestimated and overestimated in the bilingual population, especially because there is a lack of standardized tests designed for bilinguals. As discussed in Chapter 2, we cannot expect a bilingual to perform equally in each of the two languages as monolinguals and, therefore, the normative data of monolinguals do not always reliably identify language and learning disorders in bilinguals.

Although testing bilinguals in each of their languages may seem like the ideal solution, it is not always feasible. L1s can be extremely disparate (e.g., consider the multitude of minority languages that coexist with majority or official languages around the globe), and it is unthinkable to have standardized tests and health professionals with linguistic competence in each of these languages. Moreover, bilingual children could be penalized if tested in the L1 too, since they might be less competent in that language compared to their monolingual peers. This frequently happens in migrant children who have acquired the L2 in late childhood and show a shift in dominance when they start school, relegating the L1 mainly at the dimension of orality and to informal conversations. As we will see, arriving at a more accurate diagnosis is still possible, especially by integrating common diagnostic procedures with the assessment of the bilinguals' language performance in areas that are typically impaired in cases of these disorders, the so-called clinical markers, such as nonword repetition.

Finally, it should be noted that when assessing language competence in bilinguals, it is essential to evaluate its manifestations not in isolation but within a more holistic framework that includes a careful analysis of their linguistic history. It is very important to know whether the individual is a simultaneous or consecutive bilingual in addition to the quantity and length of exposure to the two languages (see Chapter 6). Only by knowing this information will we be able to have a complete picture of the bilingual's linguistic situation that fosters a more accurate evaluation of their language difficulties. Several assessments have been developed to collect information about bilinguals' language history, among which the Bilingual Language Experience Calculator (Unsworth, 2013) and the Alberta Language and Development Questionnaire (Paradis et al., 2010).

5.2 Bilingualism and Developmental Language Disorder

Following the American Psychiatric Association's **Diagnostic and Statistical Manual of Mental Disorders (DSM-5)**, a DLD is a neurodevelopmental condition including a set of different clinical features characterized by a delay or a disorder in one or more areas of language development, occurring in absence of cognitive, sensory, motor, affective, and important socio-environmental deficiencies. DLD affects around 5–7 percent of the population (Law et al., 2000). A child with DLD displays observable difficulties in understanding and producing complex morphosyntactic structures and in phonological, morphological, and lexical competence (Leonard, 2014). At the grammatical level, the difficulties vary across languages: in English, for example, children with DLD tend to have production problems in verbal inflection omitting, for example, the third person singular -s as in (1).

(1)   *She walk.

In Italian, on the other hand, one of the most reliable clinical markers (i.e., the specific areas of weaknesses in this disorder) is the production of clitic pronouns. It has been reported that children with DLD tend to avoid producing clitic pronouns (see Chapter 2), which requires sophisticated linguistic competence. In particular, when asked a question such as the one in (2), a 5-year-old likely would respond with something as in (3), omitting the clitic pronoun and thus uttering an ungrammatical sentence (Bortolini et al., 2006), instead of producing the target utterance in (4), which is commonly uttered by typically developing children starting from age 3 to 4. The production of clitic pronouns is avoided even at the age of 7 by children with DLD, although they tend to produce sentences like (5) that are grammatical but redundant with an infelicitous construction (Arosio et al., 2014).

(2)   Cosa fa   la   bambina al   nonno?,
        What is doing the girl   to.the grandfather?
        "What is the girl doing to the grandfather?"

(3)   *Bacia.
        Is kissing
        *"She is kissing."

(4)   Lo bacia.
    pro is kissing
    *"He is kissing."

(5)   Bacia   il   nonno.
    Is kissing   the   grandfather
    "She is kissing her grandfather."

Another area in which children with DLD have severe language difficulties is the repetition of nonwords: in a nonword repetition task, they are required to repeat invented words, meaningless but created respecting the phonotactic properties of the reference language. To correctly repeat the nonword, both phonological and working memory skills are required. Phonological skills assist the recognition and therefore the articulation of the individual sounds that make up the invented words and working memory skills are needed to temporarily store and correctly reproduce the sequence of these sounds. Due to their phonological and working memory deficits, children with DLD perform worse than typically developing children, to the point that nonword repetition is considered a very reliable marker of the disorder across languages.

Given their language difficulties, it is believed that children with DLD cannot learn another language, or that bilingualism can negatively interfere with their development. This false belief, in addition to lacking scientific evidence, has particularly serious consequences for children who live bilingual situations from birth, because their parents either speak a minority language or they may each have different Lıs. It is not uncommon, in fact, that after a DLD diagnosis, parents are advised to avoid using the home language in order to focus development on the language spoken in the community. However, numerous studies have shown that depriving children of one of the two languages does not lead to any improvement: on the contrary, doing so could have very negative emotional repercussions both for the child and for the family, who will also be forced to give up a part of their cultural identity.

Instead, the results of empirical research have shown that bilingualism does not worsen the difficulties of a child with DLD. A bilingual individual with a DLD has no difficulty in keeping the two languages separate and does not show intrusions or interferences from one language to another. In fact, in a study by Gutiérrez-Clellen et al. (2008), no errors were found in grammatical structure transfer or in confusing the two linguistic systems. Bilingual children with DLD exhibit distinct difficulties in each of the two languages, while linguistic competence, both grammatical and lexical, is often similarly affected in both languages (Blacksmith & Marini, 2010; Marinis et al., 2017; Paradis, 2010). For example, similar errors were reported in English verb inflection (Paradis et al., 2003), in producing clitics in languages such as Italian and French, and in nonword repetition (Grüter, 2005). These findings suggest that difficulties are due to the presence of a DLD, and not to bilingualism, and that bilingualism does not worsen the disorder. In some cases, exposure to two languages can actually lead to benefits for impaired children. For instance, Tsimpli et al. (2017) found that, although bilinguals with a DLD struggled with clitic production as much as monolinguals with DLD, bilinguals were significantly aided by the context of the storytelling task, outperforming their monolingual peers and approaching the level of the typically developing children.

A bilingual advantage has also been identified in tasks measuring the ability to understand mental states of oneself and others – an ability known as Theory of Mind (see Chapter 1). Bilingual children appear to perform better on these tasks due to early exposure to two distinct language systems and the need to understand which one is appropriate to use in each context (Kovács, 2009). It should be noted that the presence of DLD does not prevent a child from becoming bilingual: although learning an L2 might present a challenge, the cognitive advantages typically associated with bilingualism can be even more beneficial for these children (e.g., by favoring the development of compensatory strategies that allow them to circumvent the difficulties).

Another issue to consider concerns DLD assessment in bilingual children, especially consecutive bilinguals. As we have seen in Chapter 2, consecutive bilingual children, in addition to having a less developed vocabulary than that of monolinguals, may have difficulties in the same domains (e.g., morphosyntax) that are affected by DLD. These similarities, especially in the early stages of L2 development, can lead to misdiagnoses of DLD in bilinguals whose difficulties stem from insufficient competence in the L2 which will spontaneously resolve themselves in time. In addition to overdiagnosis of DLD, there is also the risk of underdiagnosis, that is, the tendency not to identify the disorder in children who actually suffer from it, mistakenly attributing their difficulties to bilingualism.

However, correctly identifying DLD in bilinguals is not impossible. For instance, research suggests that nonword repetition tasks, in which bilinguals typically perform similar to monolinguals, is a good way of assessing DLD, even among bilinguals in early stages of L2 development (Garraffa et al., 2019). Sentence repetition also appears to be a good indicator. More specifically, a bilingual child displaying language difficulties in their L2, but good nonword and sentence repetition skills is unlikely to have DLD, and their weaknesses are more likely related to the fact that they are still in the process of acquiring their L2. Although it remains ideal, whenever possible, to test children in both languages for a more precise result, it has been shown that the accuracy of diagnoses is high also when evaluating the individuals only in the community language (Armon-Lotem & Meir, 2016).

Furthermore, in order to avoid the risk of **false negatives** and **false positives** in DLD diagnosis, it is essential to evaluate the linguistic performance of bilinguals while taking into account their language backgrounds, such as the age at which they were first exposed to the L2 and the quantity and quality of the language input to which they have been exposed. If, for example, a bilingual child exposed to an L2 for less than two years has difficulty producing clitic pronouns but typical performance on nonword repetition, we can likely exclude the presence of DLD. This is because difficulty with clitics can be a reflection of the child's novice level of L2 competence. If, however, the child has problems with clitic production *and* nonword repetition, it is likely that these difficulties stem from DLD.

Bilingualism Matters

In Which Language Should Bilingual Children Be Assessed for a DLD?

One of the major concerns that health professionals report during the diagnosis of DLD is regarding the choice of language in which the assessment should be conducted. Although a proper assessment should always examine both of the bilinguals' languages, it should be noted that this option is often not feasible. This would indeed require the presence of health practitioners proficient in both languages to administer tests, which might be particularly different in migrant contexts that are typically characterized by a great heterogeneity and a high number of minority languages. Not to mention the fact that in some languages there are no standardized tools available for language assessment. Moreover, it should be emphasized that it is never appropriate to compare a bilingual individual to a monolingual standard. As we have already observed, a bilingual is not a sum of two monolinguals, and might thus underperform with respect to monolinguals in specific language domains.

Adjusting the norms of standardized tests is also not feasible, due to the high heterogeneity of the bilingual population in terms of linguistic background, age of onset, amount of language use, and language status. Although some progress has been made (e.g., proposing new clinical practices based on different diagnostic tools for the identification of language disorders in bilinguals or providing norms based on bilingual students), these novel developments are not yet included in clinical practice and further research is still needed. As suggested above, a promising strategy to address this issue is that of analyzing bilinguals' performance of the so-called clinical markers of DLD – the particular areas with which monolingual children with language disorders struggle and which are less affected by bilingualism, to verify whether possible differences between the two populations allow us to discriminate between them. Nonword repetition, for instance, has been reported as a rather good clinical marker for DLD across different languages, as children with DLD often struggle in this task, while typically developing bilinguals generally perform similarly to their monolingual peers.

5.3   Bilingualism and Dyslexia

Developmental dyslexia, belonging to the overarching category of specific learning disabilities, is a neurodevelopmental disorder that compromises a person's ability to read and spell properly in absence of cognitive, neurological, physical, or emotional disorders. The incidence of dyslexia is 5–10 percent and it is markedly influenced by the opaqueness of the writing system, with a higher prevalence in opaque orthographies, as English or French, than in more transparent ones, as Italian or German (Landern et al., 2013).

Although reading difficulties are the most obvious symptoms of dyslexia, other linguistic deficits have also been identified in individuals with dyslexia, especially regarding phonological competence and lexical access, as well as in tasks that place high demand on working memory and processing resources, such as comprehending and producing complex morphosyntactic structures (Nicolson & Fawcett, 2008; Ramus & Szenkovits, 2008; Vender, 2017).

Studying the interaction between bilingualism and dyslexia along with analyzing the effects of bilingualism in dyslexic children is of crucial importance, especially when elaborating a more correct and complete diagnosis of the disorder in bilingual individuals. It is known, in fact, that bilinguals can have difficulties in the early stages of learning to read and write, especially if their L2 competence is still underdeveloped and if they receive literacy instruction for the first time in their L2, as often happens to children living in contexts of immigration that are not literate in their home language. However, these literacy difficulties are often linked to exposure to and competence in the children's vehicular language, especially with respect to their vocabulary, which is generally less rich than that of their monolingual peers, and they typically disappear after the first two years of education (August & Shanahan, 2006).

If a bilingual child is diagnosed with dyslexia, a main concern that caregivers and teachers, among others, have is whether to continue using both languages or to discourage it. Unfortunately, it is often mistakenly believed that managing two language systems can exacerbate the difficulties caused by dyslexia, and consequently, families are advised to abandon their mother tongue, in order to permit better development of the language used in school. However, numerous studies have shown that bilingualism does not worsen dyslexia. Importantly, it has been shown that biliterate bilinguals with dyslexia are able to develop different reading strategies in their languages, depending on the nature of the writing systems, without showing signs of confusion and even displaying advantages with respect to their monolinguals peers (Klein et al., 2003; Lallier et al., 2018).

Although research on the relationship between bilingualism and dyslexia is still in its infancy, experimental evidence suggests that being exposed to two languages does not have a negative effect on dyslexia. In phonological awareness, for instance, bilinguals with dyslexia show a similar performance to monolinguals with dyslexia, especially in nonword repetition, which also appears to be particularly suitable for integrating diagnostic batteries and leading to a more accurate identification of dyslexia in both bilinguals and monolinguals (Vender et al., 2019).

On the contrary, bilingualism can lead to considerable advantages for individuals with dyslexia. Siegel (2016) studied reading skills in monolingual and bilingual children diagnosed with dyslexia. The monolingual children spoke English and the bilingual children spoke either Portuguese, Arabic, or Italian as their L1 and had been learning L2 English for five years in a school where English is the language of instruction. The results showed that bilingual children with dyslexia had better performance in English reading than their monolingual peers with dyslexia. Research by Kovelman et al. (2016) also reveals that learning a L2 with a transparent sound-to-spelling system such as Italian or Spanish can even improve L1 reading skills among individuals with dyslexia in English L2: according to the authors, learning to read in a simpler writing system permits to transfer the principles of reading to the more complex system.

Furthermore, it has been shown that the bilingual advantage observed in metalinguistic and morphological competence and executive functions extends, sometimes even to a larger degree, to individuals with dyslexia. Vender et al. (2018) report that both dyslexic bilinguals and typically developing bilinguals perform better than monolingual peers in a nonword pluralization task (see Chapter 2). In the study, masculine and feminine non-Italian words were presented in singular forms (e.g., *la nave*, "the ship") and participants were asked to make them plural (e.g., *le navi*, "ships"). Results showed that monolinguals performed more poorly than bilinguals, tending to keep word endings in nonwords (e.g., *la forde*) unchanged, without applying the correct morphological rule (e.g., producing *le forde* instead of *le fordi*). Bilinguals, on the other hand, applied the rule significantly more correctly: more particularly, it seems that they are suppressing the tendency to produce the feminine plural in -e, which is more common in Italian, sticking to the relevant morphological rule more efficiently than their monolingual peers. Moreover, it is surprising to note that dyslexic bilinguals performed even better than typically developing monolinguals. Similar advantages among bilingual children with dyslexia have also been shown in executive function tasks, such as the Simon task (Vender et al., 2019).

The studies conducted so far have shed important light on the diagnosis of dyslexia in bilinguals. As argued above, due to the possible literacy difficulties of bilingual children, correctly assessing dyslexia in L2 and bilingual children is a challenging issue. First and foremost, it is essential to consider the complete language background and current linguistic situation of bilinguals, including aspects such as the age at which they were first exposed to the L2, the quantity and quality of L2 input received, their level of L1 literacy (if any), and the distance between the L1 and L2 orthographic and spelling systems. Furthermore, it is important to carefully consider the reading difficulties also from a qualitative point of view: a closer look at reading performance of typically developing bilinguals reveals that they show different difficulties compared to those displayed by monolinguals with dyslexia. For instance, monolinguals with dyslexia tend to read both words and nonwords slower and more incorrectly than typically developing monolingual children, while bilingual children without dyslexia tend to struggle more in reading words, even though they are as accurate as monolinguals with nonwords (Murineddu et al., 2006; Scortichini et al., 2012). This discrepancy between words and nonwords is likely to be related to the bilinguals' lower vocabulary: having a less rich vocabulary, they indeed tend to struggle more than monolinguals when reading less frequent words that are not familiar to them. In light of this, an appropriate assessment should rely more on nonword reading tasks in which monolinguals and bilinguals are "on the same field" and bilinguals cannot be penalized for their less developed lexicon. A bilingual who presents difficulties only in reading real words but not when reading nonwords is unlikely to have dyslexia, as both word and nonword reading are typically impaired in this disorder, but instead, their difficulties are likely due to an underdeveloped vocabulary and a still relatively underdeveloped linguistic L2 competence. This also indicates that proposing interventions aiming to strengthen bilinguals' vocabulary can constitute an important strategy to improve their decoding skills, as well as their reading comprehension.

Finally, it can be very useful to combine classic diagnostic tests with other assessments of language competence. For example, nonword repetition has been reported as a good indicator that is able to identify dyslexia in both monolingual and bilingual children. As argued above, severe deficits in nonword repetition are observed in dyslexics, both monolinguals and bilinguals, whereas typically developing bilinguals perform similarly to their monolingual peers. Therefore, if a bilingual child shows reading difficulties, especially in reading words compared to nonwords, but does not manifest problems in repeating nonwords orally, their weaknesses in decoding are unlikely related to dyslexia. Instead, these struggles are more likely due to low language competence and vocabulary in the vehicular language. Taken together, these practices can help reduce the occurrence of false negatives and false positives, leading to a more effective identification of dyslexia in bilinguals.

5.4   Bilingualism and Autism Spectrum Disorders

Autism spectrum disorder (ASD), as defined in the DSM-5, is a neurodevelopmental condition that includes a group of disorders characterized by persistent difficulties in social communication and social interaction across multiple contexts. ASD is also associated with repetitive patterns of behavior, interests, or activities that can cause clinically significant impairments in social, occupational, or other important areas of current functioning. As a common trait, individuals with ASD have troubles with emotional reciprocity – a reduced interest in people, conversation, and sharing emotions. They also have difficulty in using and understanding nonverbal communication and in regulating their own behavior based on the demands of various social contexts. These problems are often associated with abnormalities in eye contact, adopting repetitive behaviors, resisting changes in routines, and hyper- or hypo-reacting to sensory stimuli such as temperature, pain, brightness, and smell.

Given the close connection between ASD and communication, the importance of disseminating correct information about it with respect to bilingualism is evident. Unfortunately, as we have seen in the disorders discussed so far, the myth that exposure to two linguistic systems could worsen communication difficulties looms, and families are often advised to simplify the children's linguistic environment, thus adopting a monolingual approach. However, a growing body of research suggests that bilingualism has no adverse effect on the linguistic development of a child with ASD. Hambly and Fombonne (2012), for example, found that early language development and milestones in vocabulary growth were similar for monolingual and bilingual children with ASD aged 3 to 6 and with various combinations of L1s and L2s, including English, French, Spanish, Italian, Chinese, Romanian, Farsi, and Tamil. A study by Petersen et al. (2012) also revealed that simultaneous English-Mandarin and English-Cantonese bilinguals with ASD aged 4–6 showed no difference in English vocabulary compared to monolingual peers with ASD. In fact, when considering words in both languages, the bilingual children demonstrated a larger vocabulary.

Furthermore, exposure to two languages does not hamper social development of children with ASD (Ohashi et al., 2012), nor does it worsen **pragmatic competence**, that is, the ability to use language appropriately depending on the conversational context (Reetzke et al., 2015). On the contrary, bilingualism appears to mitigate difficulties in executive functions, resulting in improved verbal skills. For example, Gonzalez-Barrero and Nadig (2019) reported better performance in bilinguals with ASD in the **Dimensional Change Card Sort** (DCCS) task (Zelazo, 2006) compared to monolingual peers with ASD. The DCCS is a test in which individuals are asked to sort a series of bivalent cards, first according to the color of the object appearing on the cards, and then according to the object appearing on them. Switching costs can be measured when individuals switching from following one rule to another. Children with ASD have been found impaired in this task and, more generally, in set-shifting activities (Leung & Zakzanis, 2014). Several studies instead have highlighted an advantage in the DCCS task among neurotypical bilinguals, suggesting that using two languages can improve cognitive flexibility (Barac & Bialystok, 2012; Bialystok, & Herman, 1999; Carlson & Meltzoff, 2008; see Chapter 3). Gonzalez-Barrero and Nadig (2019) thus extended this result, showing that the bilingual advantage is observed also in the presence of ASD, suggesting that bilingualism, therefore, can stimulate compensatory mechanisms that might lessen the difficulties associated with ASD. Benefits of bilingualism have been found in narrative production as well in structure complexity, use of adverbial cues, and accuracy of referential expressions (Peristeri et al., 2020).

In sum, experimental evidence which takes into account factors such as age, nonverbal intelligence, socio-economic status, type of intervention received, and different language combinations suggests that exposure to two languages does not cause additional deficits in language development or in social behavior of children with ASD, indicating that bilingualism should not be abandoned. It must also be noticed that depriving input in an additional language for children with ASD, in fact, not only risks impoverishing linguistic input but may also worsen some of the symptoms associated with the disorder, such as social isolation within the linguistic environment and in particular that of the family. Consequently, the children may find themselves having to communicate at home in a language that feels less natural, thus contributing to feelings of discomfort and detrimentally affecting the psychological well-being of the whole family (Howard et al., 2021; Kremer-Sadlik, 2005).

5.5   Bilingualism and Hearing Loss

Hearing loss is due to damage to the inner ear, the cochlea, in which the transfer of sound to the acoustic nerve is hindered. Among the most common treatments for improving hearing functions are hearing aids, mainly used in cases of mild hearing loss, and cochlear implants, more suitable for more severe hearing loss. The latter is a surgically implanted device with the aim of bypassing the damaged part of the cochlea to directly stimulate the acoustic nerve: if the hearing aid is limited to amplifying the sound, the cochlear implant, on the other hand, converts it into electrical impulses by simulating natural hearing.

In clinical practice of hearing loss, we again encounter the false belief that for children with cochlear implants or hearing aids, exposure to two languages will "divide" their linguistic resources and negatively affect their linguistic development. Also in this case, however, studies indicate that bilingualism does not negatively affect language development. Thomas et al. (2008), for example, report similar performance in different language measures including speech perception and both listening and expressive communication in monolingual and bilingual children who had undergone cochlear implant surgery. The children were between 11 months and 6 years old when they were first tested, with subsequent testing occurring 6, 12, 24, and 36 months after the implant. Similar findings were reported by Bunta and Douglas (2013), who found that L1 skills were commensurable among 4-year-old English-Spanish bilinguals and monolingual English with cochlear implants or hearing aids. Moreover, the bilinguals demonstrated similar proficiency in both languages, suggesting that exposure to an L2 does not hinder L1 development, but instead, can reinforce it.

Setting up a rehabilitation program that targets both languages can thus offer benefits. Bunta et al. (2016) found better performance among English-Spanish bilinguals with cochlear implants or hearing aids who had received treatment in both languages compared to bilinguals who only received treatment in English. The authors suggest active involvement of parents who should also be taught strategies in the family language that they can use in parallel with the rehabilitation program conducted by health professionals in the two languages.

In sum, the experimental evidence suggests that limiting linguistic input to one language for individuals with hearing loss is not appropriate in situations where exposure to more than one language is possible. In fact, the richer the linguistic exposure, the stronger the competence will be in the two languages. However, there are also studies that recommend greater caution, stressing the need to provide bilingual input that is as equal as possible in both languages, and insisting on the importance of parental involvement in the family language throughout treatment (Deriaz et al., 2014).

5.6   Bilingualism and Down Syndrome

The chromosomal condition caused by the presence of an extra copy of chromosome 21 (three copies instead of two, making it also called "trisomy 21") is **Down syndrome** (DS). DS is the most common chromosomal abnormality found in humans and is congenital, but not hereditary. It is characterized by a cognitive deficit associated with specific physical characteristics and growth delays. At the linguistic level, there are marked difficulties that are more severe than one would expect considering that DS is a type of nonverbal intellectual deficit. But not all areas of linguistic competence are equally affected. For example, receptive vocabulary is generally unaffected, while morphosyntactic competence, especially in production, is severely hampered. Although a difference between expressive and receptive abilities is also found in bilinguals with typical language development, the gap is much larger in cases of DS (Chapman, 1995; Kay-Raining Bird et al., 2005).

Although it may seem reasonable to ask whether exposure to two languages has negative effects for individuals with DS, the research conducted, albeit limited so far, indicates that simultaneous bilingualism does not hinder the linguistic development in cases of DS and that L2 learning at a later age is also quite possible. Vallar and Papagno (1993) reported the case of a 23-year-old woman with DS who was not only an Italian-English-French trilingual, but who had satisfactory communication skills in all three languages. Kay-Raining Bird and colleagues (2005) analyzed the linguistic development of bilinguals with DS at the chronological age of 6 years and mental age of 2 years and 7 months. All children had been exposed to both languages consistently on a prolonged basis. Compared with two groups of monolinguals with and without DS of the same mental age, bilinguals have been shown to have both productive and receptive vocabulary similar to that of typically developing children, and difficulties in producing sentences similar to those of monolinguals with DS. The bilinguals were therefore able to acquire both languages, with performance correlating to the amount of exposure and use of the languages. The identified deficits were of the same type of severity, but not worse than those of monolingual peers in each of the two languages (Cleave et al., 2014; Edgin et al., 2011; Feltmate & Kay-Raining Bird, 2008).

Burgoyne et al. (2016) also examined literacy development in individuals with DS and reported similar findings. They discussed a case study following a Russian-English bilingual girl longitudinally from 6 to 10 years old. During this period, the findings showed that in addition to having the same linguistic difficulties as monolinguals with DS, the child had good reading skills in both languages, similar to those of age-matched children with typical language development. Although children with DS can learn to read relatively well, despite presenting difficulties in understanding the text, only 8 percent manage to reach the norm of their peers: the girl who took part in this study, compared in reading in English L2 with fifty-one English monolinguals with DS, actually performed better than 91 percent of them. Although this result should be taken with caution given that it is based on a single case study, it can still be said that exposure to two languages does not appear to be an obstacle for literacy development, even when the two languages have different alphabetic systems. It should therefore be discounted that bilingualism can have negative developmental consequences for individuals with DS. Both monolingual and bilingual individuals with DS will indeed show similar types of language errors, but these will vary according to the nuances of each language.

Bilingualism must thus be encouraged in individuals with Down syndrome as well, especially when both languages are present in the home environment: discouraging the maintenance of the two languages could have negative effects, inducing a sense of isolation in the child and altering natural family relationships.

5.7   Bilingualism and Aphasia

In this section, we discuss **aphasia**, a disorder that differs from the others we have discussed so far in that it arises from damage to certain brain regions, affecting the linguistic competence of individuals who had not shown impairments before the traumatic event. For this reason, aphasia is an acquired disorder rather than developmental. Aphasia is defined as a partial or complete loss of language skills due to injury to neural areas responsible for language processing. Brain damage can be caused by a neurological trauma arising from a stroke, head injury, or infection. The extent and characteristics of the deficit are highly variable across patients, yielding to different types of aphasia. In the case of **Wernicke's aphasia**, in which neurological damage is localized in an area of the left temporal lobe known as Wernicke's area, patients have difficulty understanding both spoken and written language. They are able, however, to speak and write fluently, although the sentences are often incomprehensible because they are not able to monitor their own language production.

In **Broca's aphasia**, in which brain damage is in the left frontal lobe, in a region known as Broca's area, the opposite occurs: patients have a relatively intact ability to understand language (albeit with grammatical errors, as discussed in Garraffa & Grillo, 2008), but have severe difficulties producing language given their challenges in word retrieval. So, speaking and writing is very slow, choppy, and effortful. In other cases, there may be a loss in the ability to remember the name of objects (a condition known as **anomia**), or in the ability to repeat words or phrases (**conduction aphasia**), while in the most severe form of aphasia, **global aphasia,** both expressive and receptive abilities are compromised due to brain damage in both the left frontal and temporal lobes. Moreover, prognosis and patterns of recovery can be highly diversified, depending on the severity of brain damage, specific site of the lesion, type of treatment, and response of the patient, as well as on other individual characteristics such as age, level of education, and general health.

The extent of damage and recovery patterns in bilingual aphasics have been the subject of numerous studies since the end of the nineteenth century, and the similarities and differences, both in the impairment and in the rehabilitation of the two languages, can offer detailed information about the relationship between the two languages in the brain (whether there are separate or shared neural mechanisms) and, more generally, about the organization of languages in the bilingual brain.

Bilinguals with aphasia may show similar or different degrees of impairment in the two languages: impairments can be similar in severity in both languages, more marked in one language, or even limited to only one language. Ku et al. (1996), for example, report on the case of a 16-year-old Chinese speaker who arrived in the United States at the age of 10 and who, after suffering from encephalitis, lost both productive and receptive abilities in English, but not in Chinese. Fabbro and Paradis (1995), on the other hand, present cases of four patients who showed lower grammatical competence in their dominant or native language compared to the language which was non-native or nondominant for them. In most cases, however, language impairment in bilingual aphasia affects both languages: in a review of 132 studies, Paradis (2001) found that 61 percent of aphasics showed parallel impairment and recovery patterns in both languages, while only 18 percent demonstrated different degrees of impairment in the two languages. However, less typical patterns were also observed: 9 percent of the patients had blended impairment, mixing features of their languages, while 7 percent of patients, for example, showed selective recovery patterns, in which only one language improved, and 5 percent showed improvement in one language only after completely recovering the other language.

Another characteristic that might be observed in bilingual aphasics concerns mixing the two languages, which can be more common and also occur in the presence of people who do not speak one of the two languages, contrarily to what typically happens, since, as we saw in Chapter 1, codeswitching follows precise rules and bilinguals are generally aware of when and how it is appropriate. The mixing of the two languages in bilinguals with aphasia may be due to a problem in attentional control, that determines which language should be used and which one should be inhibited in each situation according to contextual needs. However, this atypical pattern of codeswitching may also be due to the fact that bilingual aphasics might rely on both languages to compensate for their difficulties in word finding and communicating.

It is important to underscore that, due to the large variability in the clinical symptoms of aphasia and the rather inconsistent findings, we are not yet able to give precise answers on the nature of the interaction between bilingualism and aphasia. One of the reasons lies in the fact that, although aphasia in bilinguals has been studied for more than a century, most of the research has reported on single case studies, which can be subject to great variability. Only recently have researchers begun to conduct studies on groups of aphasics and meta-analyses of the literature that allow us to have a more comprehensive understanding of the phenomenon. Another issue is that, often, detailed information is lacking about the bilingual patient's competence in the two languages prior to the onset of aphasia, as this information is not typically assessed, say at one's yearly physical. Because of this, self-assessments and reports from families are often collected after the brain damage, but they cannot be considered objective and sufficiently reliable to gather a complete picture of the patient's former linguistic skills.

In a recent meta-analysis on language impairment in bilingual aphasia, Kuzmina and colleagues (2019) found that L1 skills are generally better preserved than L2 skills, especially if the latter was learned after age 7. If exposure to the L2 starts earlier, however, there appears to be no significant differences between the impairment observed in the two languages. This suggests that languages acquired at an early age enjoy a unique status and are likely processed differently than languages learned later (Giussani et al., 2007). Proficiency level in the two languages, on the other hand, has a lesser effect: aphasics who had better L1 performance or equal performance in both languages seem to have better preserved L1 skills, while only in cases in which the patient had achieved better competence in the L2 were the deficits less extensive in the L2 compared to the L1. Similarly, patients who used their L1 more frequently performed better in this language, while those who used their L2 more often performed similarly in both languages. The results of Kuzmina et al.'s (2019) metanalysis also found that studies have consistently reported no effects of linguistic similarity on bilingual aphasics' overall performance, showing that the degree of typological similarity between the two languages plays a smaller role (if any) than language proficiency and use (Kastenbaum et al., 2019; Munoz & Marquardt, 2003).

Although fewer studies have focused on the treatment methods for bilingual aphasic patients, the preliminary evidence suggests that both rehabilitation in the L1 and in the L2 can lead to effective results (see Faroqi-Shah et al., 2010, for a systematic review of the literature). This suggests that, in the event that it is not possible to offer treatment in an L1, it is not contraindicated to do so in the L2. This applies both to bilinguals who have learned their L2 at an earlier and at a later age. Studies conducted on acquired aphasia in bilingual children have also highlighted parallel recovery of the two languages regardless of the language used in rehabilitation (Crescentini & Fabbro, 2014).

Although research on aphasia among bilinguals is ongoing, it is possible to state that exposure to two linguistic systems does not create additional difficulties for aphasics. In fact, some studies have highlighted a possible positive effect of bilingualism on recovery outcomes. Penn et al. (2010), for example, reported better performance in bilingual compared to monolingual aphasics in tasks that require greater executive control and management of conversational strategies, thus suggesting that bilingualism may offer the possibility for a quicker recovery from aphasia.

Bilingualism Matters

Why a Minority Language Should Never Be Sacrificed

The belief that dual language exposure might be harmful for children with language impairments is unfortunately still quite widespread. It is of the utmost importance to emphasize that, besides lacking scientific support, renouncing the minority language can lead to situations of great discomfort, endangering the psychological well-being of the children and their family. Adopting a monolingual approach in dealing with language-impaired children will not lead to better proficiency in the community language, but rather, it might deteriorate quality of family conversations and interactions. It frequently happens, indeed, that the home language is the only means of communication in families with a migrant background. And in these situations, parents might lack the necessary proficiency to fluently speak in the majority language and end up providing their children with a poor-quality input. Their limited fluency and fear of passing grammatical mistakes to the child might indeed hinder communication and reduce opportunities for parent–child interaction, causing the child to isolate from the family environment and their social and cultural community life, while also preventing other siblings from growing bilingual as well. Families should instead be advised to continue to use the family language, offering their children a rich, high-quality, and diversified input, not only orally, but also written so as to encourage early home literacy environment practices. This will allow a harmonious bilingual growth of children and strengthen family bonds, while also maintaining cross-generational relationships and preserving cultural heritage.

5.8 Bilingualism Is Always an Opportunity To Be Seized

Families and society are now increasingly aware of the importance of bilingualism and the benefits associated with it. However, when faced with situations involving a language disorder, the fear of worsening an already delicate situation tends to prevail. It is thus particularly important to emphasize that scientific evidence, as reported in this chapter, shows that these concerns, although understandable, are unfounded. In no case can bilingualism worsen language difficulties caused by DLD, developmental dyslexia, Down syndrome, hearing loss, or aphasia. Instead, it can lead to linguistic, cognitive, and sociocultural benefits.

As we have mentioned in this chapter, it is important to take into consideration the environment in which bilinguals live, remembering that in some cases, bilingualism is an essential component for family dynamics. Several issues can arise when giving up the family language in which the parents, for example, come from a migrant background and have learned the community language only as adults, without formal education and without having reached a very high level of competence, or in which one of the caregivers has not (yet) learned the L2. Encouraging these families to abandon their L1 in order to supposedly improve L2 development not only has no scientific basis, but can create uncomfortable situations within the family. For instance, caregivers who want to cuddle or to scold their children in a language they know very little of may be unable to express their feelings properly and get frustrated.

Research has also shown that in none of the disorders discussed in this chapter is it harmful to expose a child to an L2, even at an older age. Learning additional languages is always an enriching experience, which does not hinder the linguistic development of the L1, nor does it worsen clinical manifestations of disorders. On the contrary, bilingualism can bring lifelong benefits.

Finally, we must not forget that bilingualism can also offer greater opportunities in one's profession. Even in the case of a disorder such as schizophrenia, bilingualism can generate positive effects, even acting as a form of rehabilitation. Although typically, individuals with schizophrenia appear to have reduced employability, indeed, Seeman (2016), reported on a study conducted in Canada in which bilingual individuals with schizophrenia had a significantly higher employment rate (20 percent) compared to monolinguals (<1 percent) with schizophrenia.

Summary

Since false myths and prejudices about bilingualism and language impairment are unfortunately widespread and can be very dangerous for the bilingual's linguistic development and psychological well-being, it is essential to transmit correct information to families, but also to educators, health professionals, and society in general, making it clear that it is not harmful in any way to expose children – or people of any age – to two languages. Bilingualism, far from generating negative effects, produces multiple positive effects and must therefore always be supported and promoted.

Discussion Topics

1. Can exposure to two languages hinder the language and cognitive development of children with language disorders? Why or why not?
2. Is it recommendable to reduce the complexity of the language environment by adopting a monolingual approach with language-impaired people? Why or why not?
3. Discuss whether the advantages typically associated with bilingualism extend to individuals with language impairments.
4. Talk about whether it is possible for a bilingual child with dyslexia to learn to read in two languages, or whether it should be discouraged.
5. Elaborate on the language difficulties a child with DLD may have in both languages. Are they similar or language-specific?
6. Why is nonword repetition considered a good clinical marker for DLD across languages?
7. Discuss whether assessment and treatment of language disorders in bilinguals should be conducted in one or two languages.

6 BILINGUALISM AND SOCIETY

Chapter Objectives

- Understand how families and society can support bilingualism;
- Illustrate the role of attitudes for the bilingual growth;
- Define the concept of heritage languages;
- Discuss the importance of biliteracy and of early literacy practices in the home language; and
- Emphasize the value of all languages: elective vs. circumstantial bilingualism.

6.1 Growing Up Bilingual

Throughout this book, we have described the development of bilingual competence as a natural and effortless process, especially in the case of simultaneous and early bilingualism. We have also discussed the many advantages that bilingualism can have, even in the presence of language disorders. This does not mean, however, that it is sufficient to expose a child to two languages for them to learn both to a native-like level. In fact, it is not uncommon to find children who, despite being exposed to two languages in the home from birth, develop native-like competence in only one of the two languages, while showing only passive competence in the other. Although all typically developing children learn their native language with a success rate of 100 percent, this percentage drops considerably to around 75 percent for bilinguals (De Houwer, 2007). Raising bilingual children is also often seen by parents as a difficult undertaking that requires a considerable commitment (Okita, 2002). The most endangered language, despite what one might think, is always the minority language: all bilingual children are indeed able to learn the majority language, which is used in their community and school, while it is the language used in the home that risks attrition or abandonment.

Supporting bilinguals on the delicate path of learning and maintaining two languages may require some precautions that will help both families and societies. To illustrate, let's consider three cases of 7-year-olds Lavinia, Fatima, and Jean-Luc. In each case, the children's parents moved to a country in which a different language from their L1 is spoken five years before they were born. The children, having been exposed to two languages from birth, are bilingual.

> *Scenario 1:* Fatima is a 7-year-old girl who has been exposed to two languages since birth. Fatima's parents are native speakers of Arabic who migrated to Italy before she was born. In Fatima's home, Arabic is the language mostly used, although Fatima and her older brothers tend to speak a lot in Italian, especially among themselves. Fatima attended an Italian-speaking kindergarten and primary school, always using Italian with classmates and educators. Although sometimes she realizes that she doesn't know a few words that her peers know, she manages to communicate effectively. Within a few years, Italian has become her dominant language and she often prefers to use it at home, too. None of her classmates and teachers have ever expressed any interest in Arabic, and for this reason, Fatima tends to hide it and avoid using it when others are around, limiting it to interactions with family members.

> *Scenario 2:* Lavinia is a 7-year-old girl who has been exposed to two languages since birth. Lavinia's mother speaks L1 Romanian and her father speaks L1 English. They live in an English-speaking region of Canada where, in the home, Lavinia's mother always speaks to her in Romanian, while her father speaks to her in English. When all three are together, they

use English, because Lavinia's father does not speak Romanian. Lavinia attended kindergarten and primary school, always speaking in English with classmates and educators. Although her mother continues to use mostly Romanian with her, Lavinia, who understands perfectly, always answers her in English and in fact, has never "learned" to speak Romanian, managing to say at most a few words. Nobody at school realizes that Lavinia knows other languages and she doesn't consider it an asset.

Scenario 3: Jean-Luc is a 7-year-old boy who has been exposed to two languages since birth. Jean-Luc's parents, who are L1 French speakers, moved to Costa Rica. In the home, they always speak in French. Jean-Luc learned Spanish mainly in school, from nursery to primary school, where he always spoke Spanish with educators and classmates. Everyone at school is aware that Jean-Luc can speak two languages, and expresses great admiration for his excellent French, which he often has the opportunity to use at school during French class. He is very proud to know two languages.

The hypothetical scenarios above outline the different language histories of three bilingual children who, despite being the same age and having been exposed to two languages from birth, have completely different competence and usage of the two languages. In the case of Fatima, Arabic, the family language, coexists with Italian, the majority language spoken in the community, and Italian becomes the dominant language over the course of a few years. As we shall see, situations like Fatima's are common in which the minority language is set aside or even abandoned and the majority language is preferred and almost exclusively used. In the case of Lavinia, on the other hand, we find that there is an incomplete development of Romanian (i.e., passive knowledge of the language): even though she understands everything her mother says to her in Romanian, Lavinia does not respond in this language, for which she has developed only passive knowledge. As we will discuss later in this chapter, this difficulty can come from two factors: on the one side, the linguistic **input** which is neither rich or diversified, as it may be limited to one or very few speakers, and to a colloquial register and on the other side the lack of value or support in the community for bilingualism, which in the case of both Fatima and Lavinia, is not recognized as an important quality or an asset. A very different situation is the one experienced by Jean-Luc: not only is his competence high in both languages, but this appears to be profoundly influenced by the prestigious status of the minority language (in this case, French) in the community.

In the upcoming sections, we will focus precisely on the factors that can determine harmonious and balanced development of two languages, including the quantity, quality, and diversity of the input, the perception of the importance of bilingualism, and the attitude of the family and society toward the two languages. We will return to the situations of Fatima, Lavinia, and Jean-Luc in Section 6.6.

6.2   The Role of Linguistic Input

As is well known, the main ingredient necessary for language acquisition is exposure to the language itself. We refer to this exposure as linguistic input. The situation, however, is a little more complex: it is not enough to merely expose an individual to language in order to fully learn it. Language acquisition must include linguistic input that has certain characteristics of quantity, quality, richness, and diversification. Thankfully, for children growing up in monolingual situations, while these characteristics are still required, they do not pose obstacles for language learning. For bilinguals, the linguistic environment in which they find themselves can greatly vary and is deeply influenced by the type of exposure, the strategies adopted by the parents, the status of the language (i.e., a minority language with less prestige vs. a majority language with greater prestige), the presence of siblings, and literacy skills in each of the languages. To fully understand the linguistic histories of bilinguals and their development in the two languages in a more appropriate way, it is essential to collect this type of information, for instance through questionnaires or interviews (see Chapter 5). The factors to be taken into consideration are the amount of input, both at present and over time, the quality of the input, and the presence of educational practices in each of the two languages.

To ensure that the language is learned, it is essential that there is a sufficient amount of input. The bilingual, of course, will receive significantly less exposure to each of the two languages compared to a monolingual (e.g., in cases of balanced bilingualism, only 50 percent of input is given in each language). We have seen, however, that it is difficult to find situations in which input is *exactly the same* in both languages. In fact, it is far more likely that input in one of the two languages, the dominant one, is greater than in the other. According to Unsworth (2013), the dominant language is the one whose input exceeds 65 percent. It is essential, however, that the input in the non-dominant language be at least 30 percent, because, as discussed in Chapter 2, below this threshold, it is much more difficult to attain high competency in the language. This is undoubtedly one of the reasons why it is unrealistic to believe, for example, that a child exposed to an L2 for only one hour a week in a classroom setting can achieve a high level of competence.

To have a precise measure of the actual amount of input that a bilingual receives in the two languages, it is necessary to consider the percentage of use of each language during the day, making a distinction between the language *heard* by the bilingual and the one actually *used*. In fact, situations in which these do not coincide are not uncommon. For example, there are cases such as that of Lavinia, in which the adult speaks in one language to the child who, while fully understanding, responds in another. This phenomenon is typical of passive bilingualism, but it is also very common in active bilingualism, especially when language habits suddenly change; for instance, when a child who speaks the L1 at home starts attending school in the L2, she will begin to receive the very consistent input in this language (eight hours, or 50 percent, of his waking hours per day). In time, the L2 often becomes the dominant language and as such, leads to the tendency to use it more often even at home. Furthermore, the amount of time that a bilingual spends with family members and the language used in communicative exchanges must also be considered, as they can deeply influence bilinguals' language practices (see Box 1)

Linguistic input, in addition to being of sufficient quantity, should be as constant as possible over time. The experience of studying a language in an immersion setting for four weeks per year, for example, will have little long term effects if the individual does not practice it throughout the rest of the year. The length of the exposure must also be taken into consideration, as it allows us to explain, as we mentioned in Chapter 2, the linguistic performance of the bilingual at various levels, especially lexical and grammatical. Length of exposure also can reveal developments and any changes in the habits and linguistic preferences of the bilingual, which can vary and substantially change over time.

The time during which an individual has been exposed to language(s) can be measured by the traditional index and the cumulative index. The **traditional index of language exposure** is simple and intuitive, and is calculated by subtracting the chronological age of the child from his age when he was first exposed to the L2. An 8-year-old who was first exposed to the L2 at age 3 will have five years of exposure according to the traditional index. During these five years, however, the child will not only have been exposed to L2 input, but also that of an L1, and will have had various dynamic experiences in the two languages. The **cumulative index of language exposure** allows us to capture the length of language input in a more complex way in that it is only obtainable through a very detailed questionnaire, in which it is required to indicate which languages the bilingual uses and with whom at various times of the day (e.g., at home with each of the family members, at school/work, in extracurricular/professional activities; Unsworth, 2013). A good questionnaire also gathers information about other sources of linguistic input, such as film/television or active/passive reading. Descriptions of past language experiences are also important parts of questionnaires, asking not only the age of first exposure to the language, but also the language used in learning situations (nursery, kindergarten, primary school, etc.) and any time spent in immersion or abroad settings. Gathering a cumulative index through an in-depth questionnaire serves as a precise measure that help us to better understand the true nature of a bilingual's profile.

To give an example, let's imagine a situation in which a primary school teacher in Bulgaria finds himself working with two Albanian L1 bilingual 6-year-old children, one with very high and one with very low proficiency in Bulgarian. Both children are intelligent, work well with others, and were first exposed to L2 Bulgarian at the age of 3, at which time they entered kindergarten. Having only this information, it can be difficult for the teacher to understand why there are differences between the two children's L2 proficiency and which teaching strategies are best to use. If the teacher were to gather information using a detailed questionnaire, however, very significant differences would emerge. He would find out that although both children started kindergarten in Bulgaria at the age of 3 and spoke Albanian at home, one of them was exposed to Bulgarian for about 8 hours a day, while the other was often absent for long periods in the country of origin and attended kindergarten only in the morning, for 4 hours a day. So, we see that while the traditional index estimates the amount of L2 exposure being identical for the two children, the cumulative index can uncover marked differences that may explain the variation in L2 competence of the two children. Knowing this information, therefore, can be crucial in better understanding every individual's bilingual experience, explain any difficulties they may have in learning the L2, and inform best practices that are most effective.

In addition to being of sufficient quantity that is consistent over time, language input must also be of good quality. It must come, as much as possible, from native speakers or individuals with a high level of competence in the language in question. This is one of the reasons why it is inappropriate and counterproductive to advise a family to stop speaking the L1 with their children in the hope that there will be better development of the majority language. If parents have recently learned the language and have not (yet) developed strong competence in it, the input they will give to their children will be impoverished, with underdeveloped vocabulary, simplified syntax, and grammatical errors. Not to mention the fact that they will likely feel uncomfortable speaking this language with their children, struggling to express complex or intimate concepts. This does not mean that if parents use the majority language with their children, they will hinder their linguistic development, because children are able to filter out these inaccuracies. However, doing so not only does not facilitate the children's development in the majority language, but it also prevents them from learning the minority language. Families always should be encouraged to support and use their home language with their children, without fear of confusing them or interfering with development in the majority language. On the contrary, it is indeed the quality and the richness of the linguistic input provided to the children that matters: a bilingual child exposed to a rich and stimulating language environment has more exposure to a language than a monolingual child living in a deprived language environment (De Houwer, 2014; Hoff, 2018).

As a consequence, it is very important that the linguistic input be rich and varied; that is, it should come, as much as possible, from various speakers using different registers. Let's pause for a moment to consider the many types of language exposure that monolingual children receive – ranging from family and school contexts, to the community and other sources such as television and books. And within these settings, the types of speakers with whom monolingual children interact are also very diverse, including parents, teachers, adults of various ages and professions, and above all, other children. It follows that monolingual children are exposed to language input provided by several types of speakers and across a variety of contexts and linguistic registers, from the most colloquial to the most formal. Clearly, then, monolingual children have linguistic input that is both rich and diverse. For bilingual children, although the quantity of input in each of the languages will be lower, it is important to emphasize that input should be equally rich and diverse in both languages in order to develop adequate vocabulary and language usage skills for different situations and in various registers. This can be particularly difficult in situations in which a minority language is spoken in and limited to the home while the majority language is spoken outside of the home. Because the child is limited to input and use of the minority language that is primarily colloquial, this will be reflective in the **ultimate attainment** of the language. Ultimate attainment refers to both the final outcome or end point of second language acquisition and the ability to acquire native-like proficiency in an L2. Moreover, the most immediate consequence of limited input and use of the minority language will be that the majority language becomes the dominant one, and the minority language will have incomplete development, particularly in vocabulary and expressive abilities.

Bilingualism Matters

Home Language Practices as a Window into Children's Bilingual Development

To gather a complete picture of the bilingual child's language biography, it is fundamental to consider not only which are the languages to which the child is exposed at home and in the community, but also the *amount of time* that a bilingual spends with family members and *which language(s) are* used in communicative exchanges. For instance, think about the situation of a child whose mother speaks L1 Japanese and father speaks L1 Korean. Although all of the prerequisites needed for the child to grow up bilingual are in place, if she always uses Japanese with her mother and during school and extracurricular activities and sees her father for only about an hour a day, she will receive very little input in Korean to allow her to develop advanced competence. Furthermore, it is reasonable to expect differences in both languages compared to peers who spend the majority of their time speaking Japanese but also a few hours a day speaking in Korean. These differences are why it is futile to evaluate language competence in bilingual children based solely on the type of languages involved. On the contrary, it is also necessary to accurately reconstruct the quantity and type of input to which they are exposed.

6.3   The Role of Formal Education

Formal education and literacy in a language have the power to significantly affect the overall development of the language itself, promoting an enriched vocabulary, using more articulated sentences and with a more sophisticated syntax, and stimulating metalinguistic analysis and reflection on the language. It is evident, in fact, that the language used in formal and educational situations is considerably different from that of ordinary communication. However, both types of communication are necessary for advanced competence in the language. As initially proposed by Cummins (1984, 2008), it is necessary to differentiate between **basic interpersonal communication skills** (BICS) and **cognitive academic language proficiency** (CALP). BICS refer to the ability to communicate in ordinary and colloquial situations, while CALP refers to the competence of the language specifically used in educational settings, including access to oral and written academic registers of schooling (Cummins, 2000). Both BICS and CALP reflect different linguistic registers and each develop at different times: BICS begin to develop first, usually within one to two years, while CALP emerges later, approximately after five to seven years, and only through exposure to formal education and written language.

The distinction between BICS and CALP is relevant for an appropriate assessment of a bilingual child's schooling. In fact, the tendency to conflate the conversational and academic dimensions can have negative consequences on the proper evaluation of bilinguals' school achievements (Cummins, 2008). For instance, it might be the case that after having observed the presence of learning difficulties in a bilingual child, educators and health practitioners assume that these weaknesses are not related to their still immature language competence in the L2 based only on the fact that he managed to converse fluently and easily in the language, without considering his academic proficiency. This could lead to the unfortunate consequence that the child is inappropriately placed in a special educational program, or diagnosed with a learning impairment, in which case, he receives support that is not appropriate for them. It is thus important to distinguish these two dimensions and to address the development of the child's CALP skills, by providing learning environments that maximize their language – and especially literacy – development with extensive engaged reading (Cummins, 2008; Guthrie, 2004). We should also note that the development of CALP skills should be considered in both the majority, vehicular language, and the minority, family language. We indeed unfortunately see, especially in cases of immigration with less prestigious languages, that children are not often offered formal education in the minority language, and consequently, they will not be able to benefit from the enrichment in language competence in academic settings. This is partly the reason why children raised in this context rarely achieve the same level of proficiency in the L1 as their parents. For this to happen, there must be opportunities for higher level interaction, exposure to informal and formal registers with diverse linguistic input, and literacy competence also in the family language (Cordin, 2013). Languages spoken in the home that are different from the majority/official language of the community are often referred to as **heritage languages** and typically face challenges in becoming fully developed language systems due to characteristics of the input. Among these characteristics is the lack of literacy development which can result in quantitative and qualitative differences, for example, between a bilingual child's heritage language and what for their parents is a fully developed L1 (Rothman, 2009).

As Kupisch and Rothman (2018) point out, formal education can affect the development of a language in different ways. First, some of the properties of standard language that are part of formal registers are usually acquired in school, such as use of the subjunctive in English and many other languages. For example, compare the expressions in (1) and (2), widely used in the colloquial speech, to their "grammatically correct" versions in (3) and (4), respectively. These sentences require that the underlined verbs be conjugated in the subjunctive mood. It is less likely that an individual will learn that (3) and (4) are correct without exposure to these structures in formal, academic settings.

(1)   *If I <u>was</u> you, I wouldn't go.

(2)   *The teacher demanded that we <u>are</u> on time.

(3)   If I <u>were</u> you, I wouldn't go.

(4)   The teacher demanded that we <u>be</u> on time.

In addition, if bilingual children are not exposed to reading and writing in their home language, the chances of being exposed to standard varieties and of acquiring formal aspects of the language are further reduced. Through literacy and formal instruction, speakers are exposed to a wider variety of grammatical constructions and vocabulary that will considerably influence their linguistic development, along with fostering opportunities for interaction with different types of speakers of different ages. The lack of formal education may thus explain why bilinguals develop less grammatical and pragmatic competence in the family language.

Furthermore, the absence of literacy instruction in the home language might hinder not only the overall development of this language, but also of the community language as well. As Cummins (2000) points out, in order to make the most of environmental stimuli and master both languages, it is necessary that the bilingual reaches a minimum level of competence in each of the two languages. Once this threshold is reached, certain general linguistic and cognitive skills – specifically the mechanisms involved in reasoning and making associations – can be transferred from one language to another. This can be visually represented by a **dual iceberg** (see Figure 6.1). When looking above the surface of the water, represented by the horizontal line, it

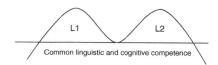

Figure 6.1 The dual iceberg representation of bilingual proficiency.

appears as though there are two icebergs. But when looking below the surface, we see that the two icebergs are actual one larger one underneath. The implication for bilingualism is that the two languages "on the inside" share the same cognitive mechanisms led by a central operating system from which both languages develop and to which both languages contribute.

The explanation seen in the dual iceberg also applies to literacy development: to learn to read and write, universal basic knowledge is required, such as the understanding that a spoken language correlates to letters that can be read and written. Once this general knowledge has been learned in one language, it can be transferred to another without needing to be relearned (Perfetti, 2003). Importantly, if literacy instruction begins in the L2, it is fundamental that children have at least some level of proficiency in this language (Soltero-González et al., 2016). When bilingual children are exposed to literacy and education in the minority language, there can be many positive benefits both for linguistic development and for reading and writing *in both languages*. While a school system in which education is provided in two languages may seem like a very difficult undertaking, it is important to encourage and incentivize the spread of early literacy and informal education practices in families as we will advocate for in Section 6.4.

As argued above, it should be emphasized that distinguishing conversational and academic proficiency can have a significant impact on the majority language used at school. Ignoring this can lead to misunderstandings about academic difficulties that bilinguals might have in the vehicular language, pretending that a child has reached a native and complete proficiency just because after some years of exposure they eventually managed to conversate fluently. Based on this inappropriate consideration, which does not take into account academic proficiency, their learning difficulties might be wrongly interpreted as lack of commitment or motivation on the part of the children.

Related to this, another misconception is to think that a person who has reached a satisfactory level in the conversational abilities in the community language is ready to tackle academic tasks, which are arguably more demanding from a cognitive point of view, without the need for additional language support (Luise, 2006). It should rather be noted, instead, that even at these more advanced, academic levels, bilinguals need specific interventions different than those used for monolinguals, since the activities proposed in the classroom typically do not focus on the acquisition of an L2, nor are they designed for individuals who have a still lower proficiency in the L2.

6.4 Attitudes Toward Bilingualism

Every language is tightly linked to culture, but languages also represent part of an individual's identity. For this reason, learning a language, especially for bilinguals, is not only a cognitive process, but also has important psychological implications. Among these are societal and family attitudes toward bilingualism and, in particular, the child's perception of the importance that is attributed to bilingualism. As reiterated several times in this book, knowing two languages brings enriching experiences and cultural and professional opportunities, as well as linguistic and cognitive advantages. But in general, when we think about bilinguals, we tend to image speakers of two **prestigious languages,** those that are normally highly regarded or viewed as particularly valuable. Within speech communities, prestige is the level of regard, esteem, and social value that is assigned to a language as compared to other languages or dialects. This prestige is based on several factors, including identification with a powerful social group, richness of literary or cultural heritage, and international standing. Bilingualism that involves prestigious languages (English, French, Spanish, etc.) that are widely used in social media and taught in schools across the world is generally highly appraised by society. Conversely, when bilingualism involves a less prestigious language, like the many immigrant languages that coexist with majority ones, attitudes tend to be less enthusiastic, even if only unconsciously. This is a phenomenon in bilingualism that often concerns both society, which tends to favor prestigious languages, and the migrant family itself, which may consider its own language of origin as less important and valuable.

This leads to the distinction between elective bilingualism and circumstantial bilingualism (Paulston, 1980). **Elective bilingualism** refers to situations in which two languages are attained through formal study of an L2, including literacy, and is considered a sign of education and high social status. This type of bilingualism most often includes languages with wide global diffusion, are recognized in school curricula, and are used in mass communications. Often, one of the two languages is "chosen" by the individual and learned in an educational context. Bilinguals who are born to parents who speak prestigious languages are considered "fortunate," given that their bilingual competence is recognized and appreciated both by society and by the international academic community, as in the case of Jean-Luc, one of the three scenarios we described in Section 6.1. In contrast with elective bilingualism is **circumstantial bilingualism**, which is often associated with working-class immigrant communities whose home language is used at home, is primarily oral, and has little to no presence in formal education. Bilingualism, in this case, is generally not the result of a choice, but rather the result of conditions and occurrences such as moving to another country where this language is not spoken. Circumstantial bilingualism is generally perceived as less prestigious than elective bilingualism, since it exists in communities where it has little social presence, is not included in school programs, and is not used by the media (Cordin, 2013).

Unfortunately, it is not uncommon that this lack of appraisal and, consequently, of support for *all languages*, regardless of their prestige, generates negative feelings in children and adolescents with respect to their heritage language, which, ultimately, they may abandon in favor of exclusive use of the majority language (Peace-Hughes et al., 2021). To prevent this from happening, it is important that both society, academic institutions, and families adopt positive attitudes and show interest in all languages. The primary thrust behind these positive changes must come from the family itself, which can really make a difference, as evidenced by two studies conducted in Israel by Tannenbaum and Berkovich (2005) and Shany and Geva (2012). Tannenbaum and Berkovich examined language proficiency and academic success among a large group of Russian-speaking teenagers who immigrated to Israel before the age of 6. The individuals had developed strong proficiency in both Russian and Hebrew, and according to the authors, they had retained a high proficiency in their heritage language because of **family language policy**, the set of linguistic habits and beliefs regarding bilingualism adopted and practiced by families. The bilinguals' parents attached a significant amount of importance to academic success and development in *both languages*. Indeed, despite the fact that the parents had learned Hebrew, they felt it was not only important to maintain their language of origin, but that their children be exposed to the heritage language in all its forms, written and oral.

Shany and Geva (2012), instead, analyzed a different situation, exploring literacy and academic success among a group of Ethiopian-speaking teenagers who immigrated to Israel before the age of 2. Unlike the Russian-Hebrew bilinguals in Tannenbaum and Berkovich (2005), the Ethiopian-Hebrew bilinguals had been exposed to their heritage language only in oral form, due to their parents' high illiteracy rates. As teenagers, therefore, the children were literate in Hebrew, but not Ethiopian, and their school performance revealed academic difficulties and failure rates twice as large as their peers. The authors attribute this problem to the lack of literacy and educational practices, even informal ones, in the heritage language at home. Without being able to rely on a solid and complete L1 in all its forms creates a disadvantage for these bilinguals, which worsens over time. The results of this study, along with those of Tannenbaum and Berkovich (2005), underscore the important role of the family environment, informal education practices, and attitudes toward bilingualism in the development of both L1 and L2.

Bilingualism Matters

Supporting Biliteracy as an Added Value for Bilinguals

Biliteracy includes thinking, speaking, reading, and writing in more than one linguistic system (Reyes, 2006). Children who acquire their family language first and are often exposed to the majority language once they enter school, generally receive literacy instruction only in the former, whereas the L1 remains limited to the domain of orality. Reaching biliteracy, however, is not only possible but also desirable, even in the preschool years. A large body of research emphasizes the importance of the **home literacy environment (HLE)** in which literacy materials are available at home and discussions can take place between parents and children about literature, for the early literacy outcomes of young children (Evans & Shaw, 2008). HLE has indeed been reported as a reliable predictor of literacy achievements, also for children at family risk for dyslexia and reading disorders (Hamilton et al., 2016). These family practices should be encouraged in bilingual settings as well, not only to facilitate their schooling, but also to grant them the opportunity to achieve biliteracy.

Both home and school environments have a crucial role for promoting biliteracy: educators and parents need to collaborate to create a bilingual literacy environment in which children are given opportunities to interact with literacy material in both the community and the family language, such as books, newspapers, magazines, and letters (Kenner, 2004). Children should then be encouraged to use these writing resources in both languages to develop an early orthographic knowledge, while also developing metalinguistic awareness in both languages. Integrating literacy practices at home, at school, and in the society gives bilingual children the opportunity to eventually become biliterate, rendering their educational experiences more meaningful and complete (Baker, 2011).

6.5 Tips for Families and Society

There are several things that can be done to promote and support bilingualism in all its forms, regardless of the nature and prestige of the languages spoken or signed (Emmorey et al., 2008). The first step is to realize that the advantages observed in bilinguals are in fact linked to the experience of using two (or more) languages. It is therefore important that societies recognize these benefits, particularly in cases in which the bilingual comes from a migrant background, and show interest in and appreciation for their L1. Support for the family will be essential: parents must be aware that maintaining the mother tongue will not hinder their child's language development in the majority language. Instead, providing a consistent and diverse, high-quality of input in the L1, both in oral and written forms, can positively contribute not only to the maintenance of the family language and therefore of the culture of origin, but also to the development of the majority language. Supporting and recognizing the benefits of bilingualism should happen as early as from the child's birth or, failing this, at least when the child begins school (or even day-care or nursery school). Unfortunately, it is often the case that when children are placed in an educational environment that uses a different language, some families begin to use their home language less or to stop speaking it, erroneously thinking that this will facilitate the child's development of the majority language.

Although several studies have been conducted on the family practices and strategies that can be adopted to support bilingualism, it is difficult to arrive at conclusive results given the complexity of the factors involved. In the past, for example, the **one person, one language** strategy was recommended, in which one caregiver speaks a majority language and the other caregiver speaks a minority language. However, this approach does not always work. For instance, the results of a large survey conducted by De Houwer (2007) showed that it is more effective to focus on the quantity and quality of input in the minority language and that the most suitable strategies are the exclusive use of the minority language by caregivers (if possible), or the exclusive use of the minority language by one caregiver and of both languages by another caregiver.

Bilingual children's output appears to be just as, if not more, important than the input they receive. In fact, it is only by using languages that they can develop and improve their competence and achieve greater accuracy and automaticity (Bohman et al., 2010). The active use of the minority language must therefore be encouraged and promoted, especially in cases in which the child has only passive knowledge of the language, as in Lavinia's situation that we discussed in Section 6.1. Indeed, it has been reported that switching from being a passive to active bilingual is possible. For instance, individuals who are typically passive bilinguals may find themselves "needing" to use the minority language when trying to communicate with someone who only speaks that language (Hurtado & Vega, 2004). In this regard, the importance of seeking opportunities for exchange and conversation even outside the home should be reinforced so that that input is more diverse and the minority language is less isolated. It is particularly useful to encourage interaction in the minority language between peers. Exposure to different types of speakers, especially if they represent different registers and different ages, is fundamental as it helps the child to internalize different linguistic varieties, regularize and generalize the input, establish phonetic and grammatical categories with greater precision, and reinforce the communicative function of the minority language.

Many associations operating in this sector also play an important role in promoting and supporting bilingualism. One of the largest of these initiatives is Bilingualism Matters (www.bilingualism-matters .org), founded and directed by Antonella Sorace in Edinburgh, which is a research-based public engagement network with over two dozen branches in four continents that promotes the dissemination of evidence-based information in support of bilingualism in all its forms and in all sectors of society.

6.6   Valuing and Supporting Bilingualism

Although for humans, language acquisition is a natural phenomenon, we must not forget that achieving advanced competence in two languages occurs along a delicate path that is affected by several factors including the exposure to and richness of the input (including both oral and written forms of the language) and the recognition and acceptance of linguistic diversity, regardless of the prestige associated with the languages involved. If one of these factors is lacking, the linguistic development of the bilingual could be incomplete or impoverished and, if the affected language is the L1/heritage language, there can be negative consequences for the majority language.

In light of these considerations, we can return to the three very distinct bilingual scenarios of Fatima, Lavinia, and Jean-Luc that we presented in Section 6.1. We noted in the case of Fatima that she was in a state of transition from speaking her heritage language Arabic to primarily speaking the majority language Italian. As we have mentioned, this is a very common and inevitable situation for those who attend a school in which instruction is delivered exclusively in the majority language. When children use a language for many hours a day in school, it is not unexpected that they prefer to use it at home as well, and especially with their siblings, who are experiencing similar feelings. Trying to correct this tendency may be counterproductive, but it is important that caregivers not give up on using the minority language, and that they continue to cultivate it by incorporating resources such as books and television programs that utilize formal registers, such as documentaries or news. Another crucial aspect that emerges from the story of Fatima is that there is substantial societal indifference toward this particular type of bilingualism, especially in the academic context. These attitudes contribute to the fact that Fatima considers her heritage language to be unimportant and something that can lead to marginalization. Consequently, she may contemplate stopping using her heritage language altogether.

The risk of completely abandoning a heritage language is particularly apparent in the case of Lavinia, who has developed only a passive competence in the language. The reasons for not having acquired advanced proficiency in her heritage language can be explained by several factors. First of all, the fact that only the mother speaks the language to Lavinia suggests that there is insufficient input, not so much in terms of quantity, but regarding its quality and diversity. As we have mentioned, it is essential that bilingual children have the opportunity to use their languages with a variety of speakers, especially with children of their own age. Furthermore, the fact that the father does not speak the mother's L1 and therefore that they must interact with one another in the majority language implies that there are limited opportunities for using the heritage language when the three of them are together. As a consequence, Lavinia may believe that because her mother can speak the majority language, and does so with her father, then it is more practical for her to speak in the majority language with her mother as well. These characteristics and feelings certainly do not support the maintenance of the minority language.

In the case of Jean-Luc, instead, we have a completely different situation, which can be regarded as "prestigious bilingualism," as discussed above, since both languages are considered valuable and esteemed and have developed in a balanced and harmonious way. He is fortunate to be exposed to very rich and diversified input in the two languages, with both being favorably viewed in the community and school. All this considered, Jean-Luc's knowledge of both languages gives him a feeling of pride that will in all likelihood accompany him throughout his life, encouraging him to maintain both languages.

Society should foster all situations of bilingualism so that they are similar to Jean-Luc's by promoting the importance of maintaining the minority, family language, independent from its more or less prestigious status. Key players in doing so are teachers, school administrators and support staff, as well as health professionals who have the important task of supporting bilingualism in all its forms. It is also essential that families themselves understand the value of maintaining their family language and provide rich and diverse input. The input provided at home should also target literacy development through reading books written in the heritage language. Introducing children to reading and writing principles in the minority language before starting school in the majority language can build understanding of universal principles of reading and writing which can be transferred to an L2 with little effort.

Finally, bilingual children must be aware of the importance of each language they speak, especially their heritage language, even if it is not used in the community. Communities and schools in particular should promote activities that celebrate and/or incorporate the linguistic richness of bilingual children, asking them to talk about which languages they use and to explain how these languages represent them as individuals. This in turn can stimulate curiosity about different languages and cultures among peers, and among the adults too (Favaro, 2011). It is therefore important to encourage children to perceive their L2 not as a difference that creates discomfort or even shame, to the point where they remain silent and marginalized, but rather an opportunity for enrichment for themselves and the entire community.

Summary

Throughout this chapter, we have discussed the many factors that affect language development in bilinguals, including exposure to input, which must meet specific requirements in terms of quantity, quality, richness, and diversity. In addition, we have focused on the importance of education in both languages and of a rich HLE in which early literacy practices are adopted by families to familiarize children with written resources in their heritage language and to give them the opportunity to become biliterate. Moreover, we have observed that all languages should be appraised and supported by the community, regardless of the prestige that is associated with them. If children do not perceive their family language as valuable and important, they are less likely to invest effort into fully maintaining it, more likely to limit its use to oral production in conversations at home, and eventually may abandon it in favor of using the L2 exclusively. It is therefore paramount that social policies, especially through teachers, educators, and health practitioners, disseminate correct information about the importance of supporting all languages, including literacy development in those languages, for deeper and more complete bilingual competence.

Discussion Topics

1. In this chapter we have observed that simple exposure to two languages is not sufficient to guarantee bilingual development. What are some of the factors that are necessary for reaching proficiency in both languages and why are they important?
2. Why is it essential to gather information about a bilingual's language history?
3. Why is it important to support biliteracy?
4. Explain the distinction between elective and circumstantial bilingualism.
5. Which language practices should be adopted by families to promote their children's bilingual development?
6. What should the role be of schools, teachers, and educators in supporting bilingualism?
7. Which language policies should be embraced to promote bilingualism in all its forms?

GLOSSARY

Acquired disorders: are those seen in individuals whose typical development is affected and/or deteriorates following brain trauma or damage.

Age of acquisition: refers to the moment an individual is first exposed to a language.

Anomia: is a type of aphasia in which an individual loses the ability to remember names of objects, that is, the person loses access to their internal lexicon.

Aphasia: is a language disorder where there is a partial or complete loss of language skills due to injury to neural areas responsible for language processing.

Artificial language: is an invented linguistic system, more restricted than a natural language, with a series of elements and rules that can be inferred implicitly or explicitly simply through exposure to it.

Autism spectrum disorder: is a neurodevelopmental condition that includes a group of disorders characterized by persistent difficulties in social communication and social interaction across multiple contexts.

Babbling: is one of the stages of a baby's language acquisition around the sixth month, in which the individual begins to produce single-syllable sounds combining vowels and some consonants.

Basic interpersonal communication skills (BICS): refer to the ability to communicate in the colloquial register in social face-to-face interactions.

Bilingual advantage: is the proposal that the experience of using two or more languages strengthens executive control.

Bilingualism: is a continuum on which speakers are able to move as a result of their exposure to and practice with the languages.

Bimodal bilingualism: is a type of bilingualism which refers to the regular use of two languages in different articulatory modalities: signed language and an oral language.

Broca's aphasia: is a language disorder in which brain damage is in the Broca's area (left frontal lobe) and the patient has a relatively intact ability to understand language, but has severe difficulties producing language given their challenges in word retrieval.

Circumstantial bilingualism: means that the second language (L2) is acquired forcedly as a result of conditions and occurrences such as moving to another country where the person's home language is not spoken. It is considered a bilingualism of low prestige.

Codemixing: refers to the transfer of linguistic elements from one language to another.

Cognitive academic language proficiency (CALP): refers to the competence of the language specifically used in educational settings, including access to oral and written academic registers of schooling.

Cognitive decline: is the natural physiological process associated with aging in which certain cognitive abilities are slowed down and become less efficient.

Cognitive reserve: refers to the internal mechanisms that allow the brain to protect itself from disease and aging.

Conduction aphasia: is a language disorder characterized by a difficulty in reproducing linguistics messages but intact auditory understanding of language.

Critical period: refers to the phase of life in which an individual is biologically more sensitive to the reception of a particular stimulus.

Cumulative index of language exposure: is an indicator that captures the duration of language input through a detailed questionnaire, in which it is required to indicate which languages the bilingual uses and with whom at various times of the day (e.g., at home with each of the family members, at school/work, in extracurricular/professional activities).

Decentralized cognition: refers to the ability of a person to see the point of view of others.

Decision-making: refers to the cognitive process of selection of one option among several alternatives based on the person values, preferences, beliefs, and language.

Developmental disorder: refers to a disorder that is present in the individual from birth.

Diagnostic and Statistical Manual (DSM) of Mental Disorders: now in its fifth edition (DSM-5), is one of the most well-known references for mental or psychopathological disorders used by psychiatrists, psychologists, and doctors all over the world. It serves as a reference point for both clinical practice and scientific research.

Diffusion Tensor Imaging (DTI): is a neuroimaging technique that makes it possible to visualize bundles of fibers in the brain, estimating their location and orientation. Its use has both clinical applications (identifying specific injured fiber sections or the position of tumors) and research applications (generating hypotheses on the connections and relative functions of different areas).

Dimensional Change Card Sort: is a test in which individuals are asked to sort a series of bivalent cards, first according to the color of the object appearing on the cards, and then according to the object appearing on them.

Dorsal pathway: also known as *where pathway*, stretches from the visual cortex in the occipital lobe forward into the parietal lobe. It integrates the auditory and motor systems, that is, it encodes sounds and converts them into motor articulatory planes for decoding.

Down syndrome: refers to a developmental condition caused by the presence of an extra copy of chromosome 21 (three copies instead of two, making it also called "trisomy 21"). It is characterized by a cognitive deficit associated with specific physical characteristics and growth delays.

Dual iceberg: is a graphic that represents the interaction of two languages in bilinguals' brains, in which two languages "on the inside" share the same cognitive mechanisms led by a central operating system from which both languages develop and to which both languages contribute.

Early consecutive bilingual: refers to an individual who has learned more than one language during childhood, but not from birth.

Electroencephalography (EEG): is a technology used to record multiple brain signals and requires the recording of many stimuli and precise hypotheses on the event process. EEG measures the differences in the electrical potential of different areas of the brain during an event and outputs this activity as an ERP.

Elective bilingualism: refers to situations in which two languages are attained through formal study of an L2, including literacy, and is considered a sign of education and high social status.

Event-related potential (ERP): is a physiological response of the brain to an event that is displayed by an EEG as a waveform.

Executive control: refers to the cognitive ability that allows individuals to flexibly regulate their thoughts and actions to serve adaptive, goal-directed behavior.

Executive functions: refer to a set of mental processes (planning, control, coordination, monitoring, and engaging other cognitive processes, etc.) that are responsible for the cognitive control of behavior.

Eye-tracking: is a method that allows researchers to record participants' eye movements as they process visual stimuli.

False negative: occurs when an individual who, despite suffering from a specific disorder, is not identified as such, due to poor or inappropriate diagnostics.

False positive: occurs when an individual is incorrectly diagnosed with a specific disorder due to poor or inappropriate diagnostics.

Family language policy: refers to the explicit and overt planning of language use within the home and among family members.

Functional magnetic resonance imaging (fMRI): is a non-invasive neuroimaging technique with high spatial and temporal resolution. The fMRI is able to examine the functionality of an organ because it verifies the connections between the activation of the brain and the task that a participant performs during the scan.

Global aphasia: is a language disorder caused by damage to the parts of your brain that control language in which expressive and receptive abilities are compromised.

Global inhibition: refers to a form of executive control in which the cognitive system becomes used to preferring one language over another based on context and will keep the selected language active and readily accessible.

Grammaticality judgment tasks: are tasks in which bilinguals are explicitly asked to judge the correctness of sentences of varying complexity in both languages.

Heritage language: refers to a language that is spoken in the home that is different from the majority/official language of the community.

Heuristics: refers to simplification strategies or mental shortcuts that facilitate problem-solving.

Home literacy environment (HLE): refers to the set of literacy materials and oral written practices adopted in the home to strengthen and continue the use of the family language.

Hypernyms: is a generic word whose meaning identifies a broad category that includes other words.

Hyponyms: is a word whose meaning is included in that of another word.

Input: refers to the exposure learners have to authentic language in use.

Language attrition: refers to the forgetting or losing process of a native language.

Late adult bilingual: refers to an individual who learns a second language during their adulthood, attaining high proficiency levels.

Late consecutive bilingualism: refers to an individual who learns more than one language after the age of 4 but before the onset of puberty (around 8 years of age).

Linguistic processor: refers to a network of neural areas that are responsible for coding what the person wants to express and decoding what the person hears.

Magnetic resonance imaging (MRI): is a noninvasive imaging technology that produces three-dimensional detailed anatomical images.

Magnetoencephalography (MEG): is a neuroimaging technique used to map the functional activity of the brain by measuring the magnetic fields produced by the electrical activity of the brain.

Morphology: is a branch of theoretical linguistics that studies the internal structure of words and how they are formed.

N400 component: refers to an electrophysiological potential that occurs around 400 ms after exposure to a lexical violation and whose amount changes in relation to L2 exposure.

One person, one language: refers to a strategy in which one caregiver speaks a majority language and the other caregiver speaks a minority language.

Opposite World task: refers to a verbal task in which participants are asked to name numbers written on cards appearing in a single path.

Phonology: is a branch of theoretical linguistics that studies the sounds of a language as discrete and abstract elements that distinguish meaning.

Positron Emission Tomography (PET): is a neuroimaging technique that makes use of harmless radioactive tracers (i.e., active molecules that make it possible to track and produce bio-images) to generate physiological information and map functional processes. In neurology, PET is used to help diagnosis dementias and to evaluate mild cognitive impairment.

Pragmatic competence: refers to the ability to use language appropriately depending on the conversational context.

Prestigious languages: refer to those languages that are normally highly regarded or viewed as particularly valuable.

Prosodic cues: refer to suprasegmental elements of speech that represent the melodic structure of a language, including rhythm, accent, and intonation.

Revised Hierarchical Model: is a proposal by Kroll and Stewart (1994) that argues that an abstract memory exists which consists of a common conceptual storage shared by both languages and a lexical memory that is separate for words in each language.

Rhythm classes: according to their rhythmic properties, natural languages can be grouped into three rhythmic classes: (1) syllable-timed languages in which the duration of each syllable is equal (e.g., most Romance languages such as Italian, French, Spanish, but also Turkish and Yoruba); (2) stress-timed languages in which the duration between two stressed syllables is the same (like most Germanic languages, including English, Dutch, German, Russian, and Arabic); and (3) mora-timed languages are based on the mora instead of the syllable (like Japanese). In linguistics, a mora, often symbolized by μ, is a basic unit of timing that is equal to or shorter than a syllable (e.g., the syllable *ma* contains one mora, but *maa* contains two moras).

Second language acquisition: refers to the process of learning another language leading to bilingualism for adolescents and adults.

Simon task: is a behavioral measure of interference/conflict resolution. In this task, participants are asked to respond to visual stimuli by making a rightward response to one stimulus (e.g., a circle) and a leftward response to another (e.g., a square).

Simultaneous bilingual: refers to an individual who has learned more than one language in parallel since birth.

Syntax: is a branch of theoretical linguistics that studies the rules that govern the ways in which words combine to form phrases, clauses, and sentences.

Theory of mind: refers to the cognitive ability to attribute mental states to other subjects. Children naturally develop a theory of other people's minds during early childhood, attributing knowledge, intentions, and desires.

Traditional index of exposure: is an indicator that measures the effects of input on linguistic development in bilinguals and is calculated by subtracting their chronological age from their age when they were first exposed to the L2.

Transfer: is the process of replicating structures from the learners' first language when they are speaking or writing something in a second language.

Ultimate attainment: refers to the both the final outcome or endpoint of second language acquisition and the ability to acquire native-like proficiency in a second language.

Unitary Language System Hypothesis: refers to the fact that bilinguals develop a single linguistic system, that is, a unified grammar that includes words from both languages. They later begin to develop two different lexical systems but continue to apply the same syntactic rules from the dominant language to both languages. Finally, in a third stage, two distinct grammatical systems emerge in which there is full differentiation between the two languages.

Variety (of language): in sociolinguistics, a language variety, also called a *lect*, is a specific form of a language and its use.

Verbal fluency task: refers to a task in which participants must spontaneously name words belonging to specified categories.

Wernicke's aphasia: is an acquired language disorder in which neurological damage is localized in the Wernicke's area (left temporal lobe), and the patient has difficulty understanding both spoken and written language.

REFERENCES

Abada, S., Baum, S., & Titone, D. (2008). The effects of contextual strength on phonetic identification in younger and older listeners. *Experimental Ageing Research*, 34(3), 232–250. https://doi.org/10.1080/03610730802070183

Abu Rabia, S., & Sanitsky, E. (2010). Advantages of bilinguals over monolinguals in learning a third language. *Bilingual Research Journal*, 33(2), 73–199. https://doi.org/10.1080/15235882.2010.502797

Abutalebi, J., & Green, D. (2008). Control mechanisms in bilingual language production: Neural evidence for language switching studies. *Language and Cognitive Processes*, 23(4), 557–582. https://doi.org/10.1080/01690960801920602

Abutalebi, J., & Green, D. (2013). Language control in bilinguals: The adaptive control hypothesis. *Journal of Cognitive Psychology*, 25(5), 515–530. https://doi.org/10.1080/20445911.2013.796377

Abutalebi J., Guidi, L., Borsa, V., Canini, M., Della Rosa, P., Parris, B., & Weekes, B. (2015). Bilingualism provides a neural reserve for aging populations. *Neuropsychologia*, 69, 201–210. https://doi.org/10.1016/j.neuropsychologia.2015.01.040

Abutalebi, J., Tettamanti, M., & Perani, D. (2009). The bilingual brain: Linguistic and non-linguistic skills. *Brain and Language*, 109(2–3), 51–54. https://doi.org/10.1016/j.bandl.2009.04.001

Alladi, S., Bak, T., Duggirala, V., Surampudi, B., Shailaja, M., Shukla, A., Chaudhuri, J., & Kaul, S. (2013). Bilingualism delays age at onset of dementia, independent of education and immigration status.

Neurology, *81*(22), 1938–1944. https://doi.org/10.1212/01.wnl.0000436620.33155.a4

Alladi, S., Bak, T., Mekala, S., Rajan, A., Chaudhuri, J., Mioshi, E., Krovvidi, R., Surampudi, B., Duggirala, V., & Kaul, S. (2015). Impact of bilingualism on cognitive outcome after stroke. *Stroke*, *47*(1), 258–261. https://doi.org/10.1161/STROKEAHA.115.010418

American Psychiatric Association. (2014). *DSM-5 Manuale diagnostico e statistico dei disturbi mentali* (5th ed.). Milan, Italy: Raffaello Cortina Editore.

Armon-Lotem, S., & Meir, N. (2016). Diagnostic accuracy of repetition tasks for the identification of specific language impairment in bilingual children: Evidence from Russian and Hebrew. *International Journal of Language and Communication Disorders*, *51*(6), 715–731. https://doi.org/10.1111/1460-6984.12242

Arosio, F., Branchini, C., Barbieri, L., & Guasti, M. (2014). Failure to produce direct object clitic pronouns as a clinical marker of SLI in school-aged Italian speaking children. *Clinical Linguistics and Phonetics*, *28*(9), 639–663. https://doi.org/10.3109/02699206.2013.877081

August, D., & Shanahan, T. (2006). *Developing Literacy in Second-Language Learners: Lessons from the Report of the National Literacy Panel on Language-Minority Children and Youth*. Mahwah, NJ: Erlbaum.

Bak, T., Long, M. R., Vega-Mendoza, M., & Sorace, A. (2016). Novelty, challenge, and practice: The impact of intensive language learning on attentional functions. *PLoS ONE*. https://doi.org/10.1371/journal.pone.0153485

Baker, C. (2011). *Foundations of Bilingual Education and Bilingualism* (5th ed.). Clevedon: Multilingual Matters.

Barac, R., & Bialystok, E. (2012). Bilingual effects on cognitive and linguistic development: Role of language, cultural background, and education. *Child Development*, *83*(2), 413–422.

Bard, E. G., Robertson, D., & Sorace, A. (1996). Magnitude estimation of linguistic acceptability. *Language*, *72*(1), 32–68. https://doi.org/10.2307/416793

Baum, S., & Titone, D. (2014). Moving toward a neuroplasticity view of bilingualism, executive control, and aging. *Applied Psycholinguistics*, *35*(5), 857–894.

Berkes, M., & Bialystok, E. (2022). Bilingualism as a contributor to cognitive reserve: What it can do and what it cannot do. *American*

Journal of Alzheimer's Disease & Other Dementias, 37(0), 1–9. https:// doi.org/10.1177/15333175221091417

Berko, J. (1958). The child's learning of English morphology. *Word*, 14, 150–177.

Bialystok, E. (2021). Bilingualism: Pathway to cognitive reserve. *Trends in Cognitive Science*, 5(5), 355–364.

Bialystok, E., Craig, F., & Freedman, M. (2007). Bilingualism as a protection against the onset of symptoms of dementia. *Neuropsychologia*, 45, 459–464.

Bialystok, E., Craik, F., & Luk, G. (2008). Cognitive control and lexical access in younger and older bilinguals. *Journal of Experimental Psychology: Learning, Memory, and Cognition*, 34(4), 859–873.

Bialystok, E., & DePape, A. (2009). Musical expertise, bilingualism, and executive functioning. *Journal of Experimental Psychology: Human Perception and Performance*, 35(2), 565–574. https://doi.org/10.1037/a0012735

Bialystok, E., & Herman, J. (1999). Does bilingualism matter for early literacy? *Bilingualism: Language and Cognition*, 2(1), 35–44. https://doi .org/10.1017/S1366728999000139

Bialystok, E., Luk, G., Peets, K. F., & Yang, S. (2010). Receptive vocabulary differences in monolingual and bilingual children. *Bilingualism: Language and Cognition*, 13(4), 525–531. https://doi .org/10.1017/S1366728909990423

Bialystok, E., Martin, M., & Viswanathan, M. (2005). Bilingualism across the lifespan: The rise and fall of inhibitory control. *International Journal of Bilingualism*, 9(1), 103–119. https://doi.org/10 .1177/13670069050090010701

Bialystok, E., Peets, K. F., & Moreno, S. (2014). Producing bilinguals through immersion education: Development of metalinguistic awareness. *Applied Psycholinguistics*, 35(1), 177–191. https://doi.org/ 10.1017/S0142716412000288

Bohman, T., Bedore, L., Peña, E. D., Mendez-Perez, A., Gillam, R. (2010). What they hear and what you say: Language performance in Spanish-English bilinguals. *International Journal of Bilingualism and Bilingual Education*, 13(3), 325–344. https://doi.org/10.1080/13670050903342019

Bortolini, U., Arfé, B., Caselli, M., Degasperi, L., Deevy, P., & Leonard, L. (2006). Clinical marker for specific language impairment in Italian: The contribution of clitics and non-word repetition. *International Journal of*

Language and Communication Disorders, 41(6), 695–712. https://doi.org/10.1080/13682820600570831

Bosch, L., & Sebastián-Gallés, N. (2001). Evidence of early language discrimination abilities in infants from bilingual environments. *Infancy*, 2(1), 29–49. https://doi.org/10.1207/S15327078IN0201_3

Bosch, L., & Sebastián-Gallés, N. (2003). Simultaneous bilingualism and the perception of a language-specific vowel contrast in the first year of life. *Language and Speech*, 46(2–3), 217–243. https://doi.org/10.1177/00238309030460020801

Braver, T. (2012). The variable nature of cognitive control: A dual mechanisms framework. *Trends in cognitive sciences*, 16(2), 106–113. https://doi.org/10.1016/j.tics.2011.12.010

Bunta, F., & Douglas, M. (2013). The effects of dual-language support on the language skills of bilingual children with hearing loss who use listening devices relative to their monolingual peers. *Language, Speech and Hearing Services in Schools*, 44(3), 281–290. https://doi.org/10.1044/0161-1461(2013/12-0073)

Bunta, F., Douglas, M., Dickson, H., Cantu, A., Wickesberg, J., & Gifford, R. H. (2016). Dual language versus English-only support for bilingual children with hearing loss who use cochlear implants and hearing aids. *International Journal of Language & Communication Disorders*, 51(4), 460–472. https://doi.org/10.1111/1460-6984.12223

Burgoyne, K., Duff, F. J., Clarke, P. J., Buckley, S., Snowling, M. J., & Hulme, C. (2012). Efficacy of a reading and language intervention for children with Down syndrome: A randomized controlled trial. *Journal of Child Psychology and Psychiatry, and Allied Disciplines*, 53(10), 1044–1053. https://doi.org/10.1111/j.1469-7610.2012.02557.x

Burgoyne, K., Duff, F., Snowling, M., Nielsen, D., & Ulicheva, A. (2016). Bilingualism and biliteracy in Down syndrome: Insights from a case study. *Language Learning*, 66(4), 945–971. https://doi.org/10.1111/lang.12179

Byers-Heinlein, K., & Werker, J. F. (2009). Monolingual, bilingual, trilingual: Infants' language experience influences the development of a word-learning heuristic. *Developmental Science*, 12(5), 815–823. https://doi.org/10.1111/j.1467-7687.2009.00902.x

Byers-Heinlein, K., Burns, T., & Werker, J. (2010). The roots of bilingualism in newborns. *Psychological Science*, 21(3), 343–348. https://doi.org/10.1177/0956797609360758

Byers-Heinlein, K., Morin-Lessard, E., & Lew-Williams, C. (2017). Bilingual infants control their languages as they listen. *Proceedings of the National Academy of Sciences*, 114(34), 9032–9037. https://doi.org/10.1073/pnas.1703220114

Callan, D., Jones, J., Callan, A., & Akahane-Yamada, R. (2004). Phonetic perceptual identification by native- and second-language speakers differentially activates brain regions involved with acoustic phonetic processing and those involved with articulatory-auditory/orosensory internal models. *NeuroImage*, 22(3), 1182–1194. https://doi.org/10.1016/j.neuroimage.2004.03.006

Cappa, S. (2012). Imaging semantics and syntax. *NeuroImage*, 61(2), 427–431. https://doi.org/10.1016/j.neuroimage.2011.10.006

Carlson, S. M., & Meltzoff, A. N. (2008). Bilingual experience and executive functioning in young children. *Developmental Science*, 11, 282–298.

Catani, M., & Mesulam, M. (2008). The arcuate fasciculus and the disconnection theme in language and aphasia: History and current state. *Cortex*, 44(8), 953–961. https://doi.org/10.1016/j.cortex.2008.04.002

Catani, M., Allin, M., Husain, M., Pugliese, L., Mesulam, M., Murray, R., & Jones, D. (2007). Symmetries in human brain language pathways correlate with verbal recall. *Proceedings of the National Academy of Sciences of the United States of America*, 104(43), 17163–17168. https://doi.org/10.1073/pnas.0702116104

Chapman, R. (1995) Language development in children and adolescents with Down Syndrome. In Fletcher, B. & MacWhinney, B. (Eds.), Handbook of Child Language (pp. 641–663). Oxford: Blackwell Publishers.

Charity Hudley, A., Mallinson, C., Sudler, K., & Fama, M. (2018). The sociolinguistically trained speech-language pathologist: Using knowledge of African American English to aid and empower African American clientele. *SIG 1 Language Learning and Education*, 3(1), 118–131.

Cleave, P., Kay-Raining Bird, E., Trudeau, N., & Sutton, A. (2014). Syntactic bootstrapping in children with Down syndrome: The impact of bilingualism. *Journal of Communication Disorders*, 49, 42–54. https://doi.org/10.1016/j.jcomdis.2014.02.006

Conant, L., Liebenthal, E., Desai, A., & Binder, J. (2013). fMRI of phonemic perception and its relationship to reading development in elementary- to middle-school-age children. *NeuroImage*, 95, 345–346.

Consonni, M., Cafiero, R., Marin, D., Tettamanti, M., Iadanza, A., Fabbro, F., & Perani, D. (2013). Neural convergence for language comprehension and grammatical class production in highly proficient bilinguals is independent of age of acquisition. *Cortex*, 49(5), 1252–1258. https://doi.org/10.1016/j.cortex.2012.04.009

Cordin, P. (2013). With our best future in mind: Lo sviluppo bilingue di bambini con L1 minoritaria. In I. Tempesta., & M. Vedovelli (eds.), *Di Linguistica e di Sociolinguistica, Bulzoni (159–166)*. Roma.

Costa, A., Foucart, A., Arnon, I., Aparici, M., & Apesteguia, J. (2014). "Piensa" twice: on the foreign language effect in decision making. *Cognition*, 130(2), 236–254. https://doi.org/10.1016/j.cognition.2013.11.010

Craik, F., Bialystok, E., & Freedman, M. (2010). Delaying the onset of Alzheimer disease: bilingualism as a form of cognitive reserve. *Neurology*, 75(19), 1726–1729. https://doi.org/10.1212/WNL.0b013e3181fc2a1c

Crescentini, C., & Fabbro, F. (2014). *Neuropsicologia del bilinguismo nei bambini*. Trieste: Jezik-Lingua.

Crowley, C. J., Guest, K., & Sudler, K. (2015). Cultural competence needed to distinguish disorder from difference: Beyond Kumbaya. *SIG 14 Perspectives on Communication Disorders and Sciences in Culturally and Linguistically Diverse Populations*, 22(2), 64–76.

Cummins, J. (1984). *Bilingualism and Special Education: Issues in Assessment and Pedagogy*. Clevedon: Multilingual Matters.

Cummins, J. (2000). *Language, Power, and Pedagogy: Bilingual Children in the Crossfire*. Clevedon: Multilingual Matters. https://doi.org/10.21832/9781853596773

Cummins, J. (2008). BICS and CALP: Empirical and theoretical status of the distinction. In B. Street & N. Hornberger (eds.), *Encyclopedia of Language and Education* (2nd ed.) (pp. 71–83). New York: Springer.

Dale, P., Dionne, G., Eley, T., & Plomin, R. (2000), Lexical and grammatical development: A behavioural genetic perspective. *Journal of Child Language*, 27(3), 619–42. https://doi.org/10.1017/S0305000900004281

Davidson, D., & Tell, D. (2005). Monolingual and bilingual children's use of mutual exclusivity in the naming of whole objects. *Journal of Experimental Child Psychology*, 92(1), 25–45. https://doi.org/10.1016/j.jecp.2005.03.007

De Houwer, A. (2007). Parental language input patterns and children's bilingual status. *Applied Psycholinguistics*, 28 (3), 411–424. https://doi.org/10.1017/S0142716407070221

De Houwer, A. (2014). The absolute frequency of maternal input to bilingual and monolingual children: A first comparison. In T. Grüter

& J. Paradis (eds.), *Input and Experience in Bilingual Development* (pp. 37–58). Amsterdam: Benjamins.

Dekhtyar, M., Swathi, K., & Gray, T. (2020). Is bilingualism protective for adults with aphasia? *Neuropsychologia, 139*, 107355. https://doi.org/10.1016/j.neuropsychologia.2020.107355

Del Maschio, N., & Abutalebi, J. (2019). Language Organization in the Bilingual and Multilingual Brain. In J. W. Schwieter (ed.), *The Handbook of the Neuroscience of Multilingualism* (pp. 199–213). New York, NY: John Wiley & Sons Ltd.

DeLuca, V., Segaert, K., Mazaheri, A., & Krott, A. (2020). Understanding bilingual brain function and structure changes? U bet! A unified bilingual experience trajectory model. *Journal of Neurolinguistics, 56*(100930). https://doi.org/10.1016/j.jneuroling.2020.100930

Deriaz, M., Pelizzone, M., & Pérez Fornos, A. (2014). Simultaneous development of 2 oral languages by child cochlear implant recipients. *Otology & neurotology: official publication of the American Otological Society, American Neurotology Society [and] European Academy of Otology and Neurotology, 35*(9), 1541–1544. https://doi.org/10.1097/MAO.0000000000000497

Deuchar, M., & Quay, S. (2000). *Bilingual Acquisition: Theoretical Implications of a Case Study*. Oxford: Oxford University Press.

Dickson, E, Manderson, L, Obregón, M., & Garraffa, M 2021, Tracking biliteracy skills in students attending Gaelic medium education: Effects of learning experience on overall reading skills. *Languages, 6*(1), 55. https://doi.org/10.3390/languages6010055

Directorate-General for communication & European Commission (2012). *Europeans and Their Languages*. Special Eurobarometer 386. https://op.europa.eu/en/publication-detail/-/publication/f551bd64-8615-4781-9be1-c592217dad83

Dobel, C., Lagemann, L., & Zwitserlood, P. (2009). Non-native phonemes in adult word learning: Evidence from the N400m. *Philosophical Transactions of the Royal Society of London: Series B, Biological Sciences, 364*(1536), 3697–3709.

Döpke, S. (1998). Competing language structures: The acquisition of verb placement by bilingual German-English children. *Journal of Child Language, 25* (3), 555–584. https://doi.org/10.1017/S0305000998003584

Dunn, L., & Dunn, L. (1981). *Peabody Picture Vocabulary Test-Revised*. Circle Pines, MN: American Guidance Service, Inc.

Edgin, J. O., Kumar, A., Spanò, G., & Nadel, L. (2011). Neuropsychological effects of second language exposure in Down syndrome. *Journal of Intellectual Disability Research: JIDR*, 55(3), 351–356. https://doi.org/10.1111/j.1365-2788.2010.01362.x

Emmorey, K., Borinstein, H., Thompson, R., & Gollan, T. (2008). Bimodal bilingualism. *Bilingualism: Language and Cognition*, 11(1), 43–61. https://doi.org/10.1017/S1366728907003203

Evans, M., & Shaw, D. (2008). Home grown for reading: Parental contributions to young children's emergent literacy and word recognition. *Canadian Psychology/Psychologie Canadienne*, 49(2), 89–95. https://doi.org/10.1037/0708-5591.49.2.89

Fabbro F., & Marini, A. (2010). Diagnosi e valutazione dei disturbi del linguaggio in bambini bilingui. In S. Vicari & M. Caselli (eds.), *Neuropsicologia dello sviluppo* (pp. 119–132). Bologna: Il Mulino.

Fabbro F., & Paradis, M. (1995). Differential Impairments in Four Multilingual Patients with Subcortical Lesions. In M. Paradis (ed.), *Aspects of Bilingual Aphasia, Pergamon Press* (pp. 139–176). Oxford.

Fabiano-Smith, L., & Barlow, J. (2010). Interaction in bilingual phonological acquisition: Evidence from phonetic inventories. *International Journal of Bilingual Education and Bilingualism*, 13(1), 81–97. https://doi.org/10.1080/13670050902783528

Faroqi-Shaha, Y., Frymark, T., Mullen, R., & Wang, B. (2010). Effect of treatment for bilingual individuals with aphasia: A systematic review of the evidence. *Journal of Neurolinguistics*, 23(4), 319–341. https://doi.org/10.1016/j.jneuroling.2010.01.002

Favaro, G. (ed.) (2011). *Dare parole al mondo. L'italiano dei bambini stranieri*. Bergamo: Edizioni Junior-Spaggiari.

Feltmate, K., & Kay-Raining Bird, E. (2008). Language learning in four bilingual children with Down syndrome: A detailed analysis of vocabulary and morphosyntax. *Canadian Journal of Speech-Language Pathology and Audiology*, 32, 6–19.

Flege, J., Mackay, I., & Piske, T. (2002). Assessing bilingual dominance. *Applied Psycholinguistics*, 23, 67–98.

Garraffa, M., Beveridge, M., & Sorace, A. (2015). Linguistic and cognitive skills in Sardinian–Italian bilingual children. *Frontiers in Psychology*, 6, Article 1898. https://doi.org/10.3389/fpsyg.2015.01898

Garraffa, M., & Grillo, N. (2008). Canonicity effects as grammatical phenomena. *Journal of Neurolinguistics*, 21(2), 177–197. https://doi.org/10.1016/j.jneuroling.2007.09.001

Garraffa, M., Obregon, M., O'Rourke, B., & Sorace, A. (2020). Language and cognition in Gaelic-English young adult bilingual speakers:

A positive effect of school immersion program on attentional and grammatical skills. *Frontiers in Psychology, 11,* 570587.

Garraffa, M., Obregon, M., & Sorace, A. (2017). Linguistic and cognitive effects of bilingualism with regional minority languages: A study of Sardinian-Italian adult speakers. *Frontiers in Psychology, 8,* 1907. https://doi.org/10.3389/fpsyg.2017.01907

Garraffa, M., Vender, M., Sorace, A., & Guasti, M. T. (2019). Is it possible to differentiate multilingual children and children with Developmental Language Disorder? *Languages, Society and Policy.* https://doi.org/10 .17863/CAM.37928

Garrett, D., Macdonald, S., & Craik, F. (2012). Intraindividual reaction time variability is malleable: Feedback- and education-related reductions in variability with age. *Frontiers in Human Neuroscience, 6,* 101. https:// doi.org/10.3389/fnhum.2012.00101

Genesee, F., Nicoladis, E., & Paradis, J. (1995). Language differentiation in early bilingual development. *Journal of Child Language, 22,* 611–631. https://doi.org/10.1017/S0305000900009971

Giussani, C., Roux, FE., Lubrano, V., Gaini, S., & Bello, L. (2007). Review of language organisation in bilingual patients: What can we learn from direct brain mapping? *Acta Neurochir (Wien) 149,* 1109–1116. https:// doi.org/10.1007/s00701-007-1266-2

Golestani, N., Molko, N., Dehaene, S., LeBihan, D., & Pallier, C. (2007). Brain structure predicts the learning of foreign speech sounds. *Cerebral Cortex, 17,* 575–582.

Gonzalez-Barrero, A., & Nadig, A. (2019). Can bilingualism mitigate set-shifting difficulties in children with autism spectrum disorders? *Child Development, 90*(4), 1043–1060. https://doi.org/10.1111/cdev.12979

Green, D. (1986). Control, activation and resource: A framework and a model for the control of speech in bilinguals. *Brain and Language, 27*(2), 210–223. https://doi.org/10.1016/0093-934X(86)90016-7

Green, D. (1998). Mental control of the bilingual lexico-semantic system. *Bilingualism: Language and Cognition, 1,* 67–81. https://doi.org/10 .1017/S1366728998000133

Green, D. (2003). The neural basis of the lexicon and the grammar in L2 acquisition. In R. Van Hout., A. Hulk., F. Kuiken., & R. Towell (eds.), *The Interface Between Syntax and the Lexicon in Second Language Acquisition* (pp. 197–218). Amsterdam: John Benjamins.

Grimaldi, M. (2017). L'efficacia dell'istruzione scolastica nell'apprendimento fonetico-fonologico della L2: prospettive d'indagine e applicazioni didattiche. *Studi Italiani di Linguistica Teorica e Applicata (silta)*, 45(1), 109–126.

Grimaldi, M. (2019). *Il cervello fonologico*. Rome: Carocci.

Grosjean F., & L. P. (eds.) (2013). *The Psycholinguistics of Bilingualism*. Hoboken, NJ: John Wiley & Sons.

Grosjean, F. (1998). Studying bilinguals: Methodological and conceptual issues. *Studies in Second Language Acquisition*, 1, 131–149.

Grosjean, F. (2008). *Studying Bilinguals*. Oxford: Oxford University Press.

Grüter, T. (2005). Comprehension and production of French object clitics by child second language learners and children with specific language impairment. *Applied Psycholinguistics*, 26(3), 363–391. https://doi.org/10.1017/S0142716405050216

Guthrie, J. (2004). Teaching for literacy engagement. *Journal of Literacy Research*, 36, 1–30.

Gutiérrez-Clellen V., Simon-Cereijido G., & Wagner C. (2008). Bilingual children with language impairment: A comparison with monolinguals and second language learners. *Applied Psycholinguistics*, 29(1), 3–20. https://doi.org/10.1017/S0142716408080016

Hambly, C., & Fombonne, E. (2012). The impact of bilingual environments on language development in children with autism spectrum disorders. *Journal of Autism and Developmental Disorders*, 42, 1342–1352. https://doi.org/10.1007/s10803-011-1365-z

Hamilton, L., Hayiou-Thomas, M., Hulme, C., & Snowling, M. (2016). The home literacy environment as a predictor of the early literacy development of children at family-risk of dyslexia. *Scientific Studies of Reading*, 20(5), 401–419.

Hickok, G., & Poeppel, D. (2000). Towards a functional neuroanatomy of speech perception. *Trends in Cognitive Sciences*, 4(4), 131–138. https://doi.org/10.1016/S1364–6613(00)01463-7

Hickok, G., & Poeppel, D. (2007). Opinion: The cortical organization of speech processing. *Nature Reviews Neuroscience*, 8(5), 393–402. https://doi.org/10.1038/nrn2113

Hoff, E. (2018). Bilingual development in children of immigrant families. *Child development perspectives*, 12(2), 80–86. https://doi.org/10.1111/cdep.12262

Howard, K., Gibson, J., & Katsos, N. (2021). Parental perceptions and decisions regarding maintaining bilingualism in autism. *Journal of Autism and Developmental Disorders*, 51, 179–192. https://doi.org/10.1007/s10803-020-04528-x

Hurtado, A., & Vega, L. (2004). Shift happens: Spanish and English transmission between parents and their children. *Journal of Social Issues*, 60, 137–155.

Illes, J., Francis, W., Desmond, J., Gabrieli, J., Glover, G., Poldrack, R., Lee, J. & Wagner, A. (1999). Convergent cortical representation of semantic processing in bilinguals. *Brain and Language*, 70, 347–363.

Johnson, J., & Newport, E. (1989). Critical period effects in second language learning: The influence of maturational state on the acquisition of English as a second language. *Cognitive Psychology*, 21(1), 60–99. https://doi.org/10.1016/0010-0285(89)90003-0

Kastenbaum, J., Bedore, L., Peña, E., Sheng, L., Mavis, I., Sebastian-Vaytadden, R., et al. (2019). The influence of proficiency and language combination on bilingual lexical access. *Bilingualism*, 22, 300–330. https://doi.org/10.1017/S1366728918000366

Kavé, G., Eyal, N., Shorek, A., & Cohen-Mansfield, J. (2008). Multilingualism and cognitive state in the oldest old. *Psychology and Aging*, 23(1), 70–78. https://doi.org/10.1037/0882-7974.23.1.70

Kay-Raining Bird, E., Cleave, P., Trudeau, N., Thordardottir, E., Sutton, A., & Thorpe, A. (2005). The language abilities of bilingual children with Down syndrome. *American Journal of Speech-Language Pathology*, 14, 187–199. https://doi.org/10.1044/1058-0360(2005/019)

Kenner, C., Kress, G., Hayat, A., Kam, R., & Tsai, K. (2004). Finding the keys to biliteracy: How young children interpret different writing systems. *Language and Education*, 18(2), 124–144.

Klein, D., & Doctor, E. (2003). Patterns of developmental dyslexia in bilinguals. In N. Goulandris (ed.), *Dyslexia in different languages: Cross-linguistic comparisons* (pp. 112–136). Philadelphia, PA: Whurr.

Klimova, B. (2018). Learning a foreign language: A review on recent findings about its effect on the enhancement of cognitive functions among healthy older individuals. *Frontiers in Human Neuroscience*, 12 (305). https://doi.org/10.3389/fnhum.2018.00305

Kovács, A. (2009). Early bilingualism enhances mechanisms of false-belief reasoning. *Developmental Science*, 12, 48–54. https://doi.org/10.1111/j.1467-7687.2008.00742.x

Kovelman, I., Bisconti, S., & Hoeft, F. (2016). *Literacy & Dyslexia Revealed through Bilingual Brain Development*. https://dyslexiaida.org/literacy-dyslexia-revealed-through-bilingual-brain-development/

Kremer-sadlik, T. (2005). To Be or Not to Be Bilingual: Autistic Children from Multilingual Families. In J. Cohen., K. McAlister., K. Rolstad &

J. MacSwan (eds.). *Proceedings of the 4th International Symposium on Bilingualism (pp. 1225–1234)*. Somerville, MA: Cascadilla Press.

Kroll, J., & Stewart, E. (1994). Category interference in translation and picture naming: Evidence for asymmetric connections between bilingual memory representations. *Journal of Memory and Language, 33*(2), 149–174.

Ku, A., Lachmann, E., & Nagler, W. (1996). Selective language aphasia from herpes simplex encephalitis. *Pediatric Neurology, 15*(2), 169–171. https://doi.org/10.1016/0887-8994(96)00154-3

Kuhl, P., Stevens, E., Hayashi, A., Deguchi, T., Kiritani, S., & Iverson, P. (2006). Infants show a facilitation effect for native language phonetic perception between 6 and 12 months. *Developmental Science, 9*(2), 13–21. https://doi.org/10.1111/j.1467-7687.2006.00468.x

Kupisch T., & Rothman, J. (2018). Terminology matters! Why difference is not incompleteness and how early child bilinguals are heritage speakers. *International Journal of Bilingualism, 22*, 564–582. https://doi.org/10.1177/1367006916654355

Kuzmina, E., Goral, M., Norvik, M., & Weekes, B. S. (2019). What influences language impairment in bilingual aphasia? *A Meta-Analytic Review. Frontiers in Psychology, 10*, 445. https://doi.org/10.3389/fpsyg.2019.00445

Lallier, M., Thierry, G., Barr, P., Carreiras, M., & Tainturier, M-J. (2018). Learning to read bilingually modulates the manifestations of dyslexia in adults. *Scientific Studies of Reading, 22*(4), 335–349. https://doi.org/10.1080/10888438.2018.1447942

Landerl, K., Ramus, F., Moll, K., Lyytinen, H., Leppänen, P., Lohvansuu, K., O'Donovan, M., Williams, J., Bartling, J., Bruder, J., et al. (2013). Predictors of developmental dyslexia in European orthographies with varying complexity. *Journal of Child Psychology, Psychiatry, 54*, 686–694. https://doi.org/10.1111/jcpp.12029

Law, J., Boyle, J., Harris, F., Harkness, A., & Nye, C. (2000). Prevalence and natural history of primary speech and language delay: Findings from a systematic review of the literature. *International Journal of Language & Communication Disorders, 35*(2), 165–188. https://doi.org/10.1080/136828200247133

Leonard, L. (ed.) (2014). *Children with Specific Language Impairment*. Cambridge, MA: The MIT Press.

Leung, R. C., & Zakzanis, K. K. (2014). Brief report: Cognitive flexibility in autism spectrum disorders: A quantitative review. *Journal of Autism and Developmental Disorders, 44*, 2628–2645.

Liu, C., Jiao, L., Timmer, K., & Wang, R. (2021). Structural brain changes with second language learning: A longitudinal voxel-based morphometry study. *Brain and Language*, 222, 105015.

Luise, M. (2006). *L'italiano come seconda lingua. Elementi di didattica.* UTET Libreria, Torino: Università.

Madrazo, A., & Bernardo, A.B.I. (2018). Measuring two types of inhibitory control in bilinguals and trilinguals: Is there a trilingual advantage? *Psychological Studies*, 63(1), 52–60.

Maggu, A., Kager, R., Xu, S., & Wong, P. (2019). Complexity drives speech sound development: Evidence from artificial language training. *Journal of Experimental Psychology: Human Perception and Performance*, 45(5), 628–644.

Maneva, B., & Genesee, F. (2002). Bilingual babbling: Evidence for language differentiation in dual language acquisition. In B. Skarabela., S. Fish, & A. H.-J. Do (eds.), *Proceedings of 26th Annual Boston University Conference on Language Development* (pp. 383–392). Somerville, MA: Cascadilla Press.

Marchman, V., Martínez-Sussmann, C., & Dale, P. (2004). The language-specific nature of grammatical development: Evidence from bilingual language learners. *Developmental Science*, 7, 212–224. https://doi.org/10.1111/j.1467-7687.2004.00340.x

Marinis, T., Armon-Lotem, S., & Pontikas, G. (2017). Language impairment in bilingual children: State of the art 2017. *Linguistic Approaches to Bilingualism*, 7(34), 265–276. https://doi.org/10.1075/lab.7.3-4

Markman, E., & Wachtel, G. (1988). Children's use of mutual exclusivity to constrain the meaning of words. *Cognitive Psychology*, 20(2), 121–57.

Mårtensson, J., Eriksson, J., Bodammer, N. C., Lindgren, M., Johansson, M., Nyberg, L., & Lövdén, M. (2012). Growth of language-related brain areas after foreign language learning. *NeuroImage*, 63(1), 240–244. https://doi.org/10.1016/j.neuroimage.2012.06.043

Mehler, J., Jusczyk, P., Lambertz, G., Halsted, N., Bertoncini, J., & Amiel-Tison, C. (1988). A precursor of language acquisition in young infants. *Cognition*, 29(2), 143–178. https://doi.org/10.1016/0010-0277(88)90035-2

Melloni C., Vender M., & Delfitto, D. (2019). Nonword pluralization: evidence for an advantage of bilingualism in Albanian-Italian and Romanian-Italian bilingual children. In R. Slabakova., J. Corbet., L. Dominguez., A. Dudley., & A. Wallington (eds.), *Explorations in*

Second Language Acquisition and Processing (pp. 238–250). Newcastle: Cambridge Scholars Publishing.

Morgan-Short, K. (2014). Electrophysiological approaches to understanding second language acquisition: A field reaching its potential. *Annual Review of Applied Linguistics, 34,* 15–36. https://doi .org/10.1017/S026719051400004X

Morgan-Short, K., Deng, Z., Brill-Schuetz, K., Faretta-Stutenberg, M., Wong, P., & Wong, F. (2015). A view of the neural representation of second language syntax through artificial language learning under implicit contexts of exposure. *Studies in Second Language Acquisition,* 37(2), 383–419. https://doi.org/10.1017/S0272263115000030

Moro, A. (2016). *The Boundaries of Babel: The Brain and the Enigma of Impossible Languages.* Cambridge, MA: MIT Press.

Muñoz, M., & Marquardt, T. (2003). Picture naming and identification in bilingual speakers of Spanish and English with and without aphasia. *Aphasiology,* 17(12), 1115–1132. https://doi.org/10.1080/02687030344000427

Murineddu M., Duca, V., & Cornoldi, C. (2006). Difficoltà di apprendimento degli studenti stranieri. *Difficoltà di apprendimento,* 12(1), 49–70.

Nicoladis, E., & Secco, G. (2000). The role of a child's productive vocabulary in the language choice of a bilingual family. *First Language, 20,* 3–28. https://doi.org/10.1177/014272370002005801

Nicolson, R., & Fawcett, J. (eds.) (2008). *Dyslexia, Learning and the Brain.* Cambridge, MA: MIT Press.

Ohashi, J. K., Mirenda, P., Marinova-Todd, S., Hambly, C., Fombonne, E., Szatmari, P., Bryson, S., Roberts, W., Smith, I., Vaillancourt, T., Volden, J., Waddell, C., Zwaigenbaum, L., Georgiades, S., Duku, E., & Thompson, A. (2012). Comparing early language development in monolingual- and bilingual-exposed young children with autism spectrum disorders. *Research in Autism Spectrum Disorders,* 6(2), 890–897. https://doi.org/10.1016/j.rasd.2011.12.002

Okita, T. (2002). *Invisible Work: Bilingualism, Language Choice and Childrearing in Intermarried Families.* Amsterdam; Philadelphia: Benjamins Pub. Co.

Osterhout, L., Poliakov, A., Inoue, K., McLaughlin, J., Valentine, G., Pitkanen, I., Pitkanena, I., Frenck-Mestre, C., & Hirschensohn, J. (2008). Second-language learning and changes in the brain. *Journal of Neurolinguistics,* 21(6), 509–521. https://doi.org/10.1016/j.jneuroling .2008.01.001

Paap, K., & Sawi, O. (2016). The role of test-retest reliability in measuring individual and group differences in executive functioning. *Journal of Neuroscience Methods*, 274, 81–93. https://doi.org/10.1016/j.jneumeth .2016.10.002

Paap, K. R., & Greenberg, Z. I. (2013). There is no coherent evidence for a bilingual advantage in executive processing. *Cognitive Psychology*, 66, 232–258.

Pakulak, E., & Neville, H. J. (2010). Proficiency differences in syntactic processing of monolingual native speakers indexed by event-related potentials. *Journal of Cognitive Neuroscience*, 22(12), 2728–2744. https://doi.org/10.1162/jocn.2009.21393

Paplikar, A., Mekala, S., Bak, T., Dahramkar, S., Alladi, S., & Kaul, S. (2017). Bilingualism and the severity of poststroke aphasia. *Aphasiology*, 33(1), 58–72. https://doi.org/10.1162/jocn.2009.21393

Paradis, J. (2010). The interface between bilingual development and specific language impairment. *Applied Psycholinguistics*, 31(2), 227–252. https://doi.org/10.1017/S0142716409990373

Paradis, J. (2011). Individual differences in child English second language acquisition: Comparing child-internal and child-external factors. *Linguistic Approaches to Bilingualism*, 1(3), 213–237. https://doi.org/ 10.1075/lab.1.3.01par

Paradis, J., Crago, M., Genesee, F., & Rice, M. (2003). Bilingual Children with Specific language impairment: How do they compare with their monolingual peers? *Journal of Speech, Language and Hearing Research*, 46(1), 1–15. https://doi.org/10.1044/1092-4388(2003/009)

Paradis, J., Emmerzael, K., & Sorenson, T. (2010). Assessment of English language learners: Using parent report on first language development. *Journal of Communication Disorders*, 43(6), 474–497. https://doi.org/ 10.1016/j.jcomdis.2010.01.002

Paradis, J., & Genesee, F. (1996). Syntactic acquisition in bilingual children: Autonomous or interdependent? *Studies in Second Language Acquisition*, 18, 1–25. https://doi.org/10.1017/S0272263100014662

Paradis, M. (2001). Bilingual and polyglot aphasia. In R. S. Berndt (ed.), *Language and Aphasia* (pp. 69–91). Elsevier Science Publishers B.V., Amsterdam: Elsevier Science.

Paulston, C. (1980). *Bilingual Education: Theories and Issues*. Rowley, MA: Newbury House.

Peace-Hughes, T., de Lima, P., Cohen, B., Jamieson, L., Tisdall, K., & Sorace, A. (2021). What do children think of their own bilingualism? Exploring bilingual children's attitudes and perceptions. *International*

Journal of Bilingualism, 25(5), 1183–1199. https://doi.org/10.1177/13670069211000853

Pearson, B., Fernández S., & Oller, D. (1993). Lexical development in bilingual infants and toddlers: Comparison to monolingual norms. *Language Learning*, 43, 93–120. https://doi.org/10.1111/j.1467-1770.1993.tb00174.x

Penn, C., Frankel, T., Watermeyer, J., & Russell, N. (2010). Executive functions and cognitive strategies in bilingual aphasia. *Aphasiology*, 24(2), 288–308. https://doi.org/10.1080/02687030902958399

Perani D., & Abutalebi, J. (2005). The neural basis of first and second language processing. *Current Opinion in Neurobiology*, 15(2), 202–206. https://doi.org/10.1016/j.conb.2005.03.007

Perani D., & Abutalebi, J. (2015). Bilingualism, dementia, cognitive and neural reserve. *Current Opinions in Neurology*, 28(6), 618–625. https://doi.org/10.1097/WCO.0000000000000267

Perani, D., Abutalebi, J., Paulesu, E., Brambati, S., Scifo, P., Cappa, S., & Fazio, F. (2003). The role of age of acquisition and language usage in early, high proficient bilinguals: An FMRI study during verbal fluency. *Human Brain Mapping*, 19(3), 170–182. https://doi.org/10.1002/hbm.10110

Perani, D., Dehaene, S., Grassi, F., Cohen, L., Cappa, S. F., Dupoux, E., Fazio, F., & Mehler, J. (1996). Brain processing of native and foreign languages. *Neuroreport*, 7(15–17), 2439–2444. https://doi.org/10.1097/00001756-199611040-00007

Perani, D., Paulesu, E., Galles, N. S., Dupoux, E., Dehaene, S., Bettinardi, V., Cappa, S. F., Fazio, F., & Mehler, J. (1998). The bilingual brain. Proficiency and age of acquisition of the second language. *Brain: A Journal of Neurology*, 121(Pt 10), 1841–1852. https://doi.org/10.1093/brain/121.10.1841

Perfetti, C. (2003). The universal grammar of reading. *Scientific Studies of Reading*, 7(1), 3–24. https://doi.org/10.1207/S1532799XSSR0701_02

Peristeri, E., Baldimtsi, E., Andreou, M., & Tsimpli, I. (2020). The impact of bilingualism on the narrative ability and the executive functions of children with autism spectrum disorders. *Journal of Communication Disorders*, 85, 105999. https://doi.org/10.1016/j.jcomdis.2020.105999

Petersen, J. M., Marinova-Todd, S. H., & Mirenda, P. (2012). Brief report: An exploratory study of lexical skills in bilingual children with autism spectrum disorder. *Journal of Autism and Developmental Disorders*, 42(7), 1499–1503. https://doi.org/10.1007/s10803-011-1366-y

Pliatsikas, C., Johnstone, T., & Marinis, T. (2014a). Grey matter volume in the cerebellum is related to the processing of grammatical rules in a second language: A structural voxel-based morphometry study. *Cerebellum*, 13(1), 55–63. https://doi.org/10.1007/s12311-013-0515-6

Pliatsikas, C., Johnstone, T., & Marinis, T. (2014b). fMRI Evidence for the involvement of the procedural memory system in morphological processing of a second language. *PLoS ONE*, 9(5), e97298. https://doi.org/10.1371/journal.pone.0097298

Pliatsikas, C., Meteyard, L., Veríssimo, J., DeLuca, V., Shattuck, K., & Ullman, M. (2020). The effect of bilingualism on brain development from early childhood to young adulthood. *Brain Structure and Function*, 225, 2131–2152. https://doi.org/10.1007/s00429-020-02115-5

Pot, A., Keijzer, M., De Bot, K. (2018). Intensity of multilingual language use predicts cognitive performance in some multilingual older adults. *Brain Sciences*, 8(5), 92. https://doi.org/10.3390/brainsci8050092

Poulin-dubois, D., & Goodz, N. (2001). Language differentiation in bilingual infants: Evidence from babbling. In J. Cenoz & F. Genesee (eds.), *Trends in Bilingual Acquisition* (pp. 95–106). John Benjamins. https://doi.org/10.1075/tilar.1.06pou

Quine, W. (ed.) (1960). *Word and Object*. Cambridge, MA: MIT Press.

Ramírez, N., Ramírez, R., Clarke, M., Taulu, S., & Kuhl, P. (2016). Speech discrimination in 11-month-old bilingual and monolingual infants: A magnetoencephalography study. *Developmental Science*, 20(1), e12427. https://doi.org/10.1111/desc.12427

Ramus, F., & Szenkovits, G. (2008). What phonological deficit? *Quarterly Journal of Experimental Psychology*, 61(1), 129–141. https://doi.org/10.1080/17470210701508822

Reetzke, R., Zou, X., Sheng, L., & Katsos, N. (2015). Communicative development in bilingually exposed Chinese children with autism spectrum disorders. *Journal of Speech, Language, and Hearing Research: JSLHR*, 58(3), 813–825. https://doi.org/10.1044/2015_JSLHR-L-13-0258

Reyes, I. (2006). Exploring connections between emergent biliteracy and bilingualism. *Journal of Early Childhood Literacy*, 6(3), 267–292. https://doi.org/10.1177/1468798406069801

Richardson, F., Thomas, M., Filippi, R., Harth, H., & Price, C. (2010). Contrasting effects of vocabulary knowledge on temporal and parietal brain structure across lifespan. *Journal of Cognitive Neuroscience*, 22(5), 943–954. https://doi.org/10.1162/jocn.2009.21238

Rothman, J. (2009). Understanding the nature and outcomes of early bilingualism: Romance languages as heritage languages. *International Journal of Bilingualism*, 13(2), 155–163. https://doi.org/10.1177/1367006909339814

Sakai, K., Miura, K., Narafu, N., & Muraishi, Y. (2004). Correlated functional changes of the prefrontal cortex in twins induced by classroom education of second language. *Cerebral Cortex*, 14(11), 1233–1239. https://doi.org/10.1093/cercor/bhh084

Saur, D., Kreher, B. W., Schnell, S., Kümmerer, D., Kellmeyer, P., Vry, M. S., Umarova, R., Musso, M., Glauche, V., Abel, S., Huber, W., Rijntjes, M., Hennig, J., & Weiller, C. (2008). Ventral and dorsal pathways for language. *Proceedings of the National Academy of Sciences of the United States of America*, 105(46), 18035–18040. https://doi.org/10.1073/pnas.0805234105

Schmid M., & Köpke, B. (2019). *The Oxford Handbook of Language Attrition*. Oxford: Oxford University Press.

Scortichini F., Stella G., & Morlini, I. (2012). La diagnosi di dislessia e disortografia evolutiva nei bambini bilingui (L2): Evidenze sul ruolo del lessico. *Dislessia*, 3, 319–339.

Seeman, M. (2016). Bilingualism and schizophrenia. *World Journal of Psychiatry*, 6(2), 192–198. https://dx.doi.org/10.5498/wjp.v6.i2.192

Semenza, C., Franzon, F., & Zanini, F. (2019). *Il cervello morfologico*. Rome: Carocci.

Serratrice, L., Sorace A., & Paoli. S. (2004). Crosslinguistic influence at the syntax–pragmatics interface: Subjects and objects in English–Italian bilingual and monolingual acquisition. *Bilingualism: Language and Cognition*, 7(3), 183–206. https://doi.org/10.1017/S1366728904001610

Shallice, T., & Burgess, P. (1996). The domain of supervisory processes and temporal organization of behaviour. *Philosophical Transactions of the Royal Society*, 351, 1405–1411. https://doi.org/10.1098/rstb.1996.0124

Shany, M., & Geva, E. (2012). Cognitive, language, and literacy development in socio-culturally vulnerable school children: The case of Ethiopian Israeli children. In M. Leikin., M. Schwartz., & Y. Tobin (eds.), *Current Issues in Bilingualism: Cognitive and Socio-linguistic Perspectives* (pp. 77–118). New York: Springer.

Siegel, L. (2016). Bilingualism and dyslexia: The case of children learning English as an additional language. In L. Peer. & G. Reid (eds.), *Multilingualism, Literacy and Dyslexia: Breaking Down Barriers for Educators* (pp. 137–147). Abingdon: Routledge.

Simon, J., & Rudell, A. (1967). Auditory S-R compatibility: The effect of an irrelevant cue on information processing. *The Journal of Applied Psychology*, *51*(3), 300–304. https://doi.org/10.1037/h0020586

Soltero-González, L., Sparrow, W., Butvilofsky, S., Escamilla, K., & Hopewell, S. (2016). Effects of a paired literacy program on emerging bilingual children's biliteracy outcomes in third grade. *Journal of Literacy Research*, *48*(1), 80.

Sorace, A. (2010). Magnitude estimation in language acquisition research. In S. Unsworth & E. Blom (eds.), *Experimental Methods in Language Acquisition Research* (pp. 57–72). Amsterdam: Benjamins.

Sorace, A. (2011). Pinning down the concept of "interface". *Linguistic Approaches to Bilingualism*, *1*(1), 1–33. https://doi.org/10.1075/lab.1.1.01sor

Sorace, A., Serratrice, L., Filiaci, F., & Baldo, M. (2009). Discourse conditions on subject pronoun realization: Testing the linguistic intuitions of older bilingual children. *Lingua*, *119*(3), 460–477. https://doi.org/10.1016/j.lingua.2008.09.008

Soskey, L., Holcomb P., & Midgley, K. (2016). Language effects in second-language learners: A longitudinal electrophysiological study of Spanish classroom learning. *Brain Research*, *1646*, 44–52. https://doi.org/10.1016/j.brainres.2016.05.028

Stein, M., Winkler, C., Kaiser, A., & Dierks, T. (2014). Structural brain changes related to bilingualism: Does immersion make a difference? *Frontiers in Psychology*, *5*, 1116. https://doi.org/10.3389/fpsyg.2014.01116

Stern, Y. (2012). Cognitive reserve in ageing and Alzheimer's disease. *Lancet Neurology*, *11*(11), 1006–12. https://doi.org/10.1016/S1474-4422(12)70191-6

Tannenbaum, M., & Berkovich, M. (2005). Family relations and language maintenance: Implications for language educational policies. *Language Policy*, *4*, 287–309. https://doi.org/10.1007/s10993-005-7557-7

Taylor, C., Hall, S., Manivannan, S., Mundil, N., & Border, S. (2022). The neuroanatomical consequences and pathological implications of bilingualism. *Journal of Anatomy*, *240*(2), 410–427. https://doi.org/10.1111/joa.13542

Thomas E., El-kashlan H., & Zwolan T. (2008). Children with cochlear implants who live in monolingual and bilingual homes. *Otology and Neurotology*, *29*, 230–234.

Tsimpli I., Peristeri E., & Andreu, M. (2017). Object clitic production in monolingual and bilingual children with specific language impairment:

A comparison between elicited production and narratives. *Linguistic Approaches to Bilingualism, 7*(3–4), 394–430.

Unsworth, S. (2013). Assessing the role of current and cumulative exposure in simultaneous bilingual acquisition: The case of Dutch gender. *Bilingualism: Language and Cognition, 16*, 86–110.

Unsworth, S. (2013a). Current issues in multilingual first language acquisition. *Annual Review of Applied Linguistics, 33*, 21–50. https://doi.org/10.1017/S0267190513000044

Valenzuela M., & Sachdev, P. (2009). Can cognitive exercise prevent the onset of dementia? Systematic review of randomized clinical trials with longitudinal follow-up. *American Journal of Geriatric Psychiatry, 1*(3), 179–187. https://doi.org/10.1097/JGP.0b013e3181953b57

Vallar, G., & Papagno, C. (1993). Preserved vocabulary acquisition in Down's syndrome: the role of phonological short-term memory. *Cortex; A Journal Devoted to the Study of the Nervous System and Behavior, 29*(3), 467–483. https://doi.org/10.1016/s0010–9452(13)80254-7

Vemuri, P., Lesnick, T., Przybelski, S., Machulda, M., Knopman, D., Mielke, M., Roberts, R., Geda, Y., Rocca, W., Petersen, R., & Jack, C. Jr. (2014). Association of lifetime intellectual enrichment with cognitive decline in the older population. *JAMA Neurology, 71*(8), 1017–1024. https://doi.org/10.1001/jamaneurol.2014.963

Vender, M., Krivochen, D. G., Phillips, B., Saddy, D., & Delfitto, D. (2019). Implicit learning, bilingualism, and dyslexia: Insights from a study assessing AGL with a modified Simon task. *Frontiers in Psychology, 10*, 1647. https://doi.org/10.3389/fpsyg.2019.01647

Vender, M. (ed.) (2017). *Disentangling Dyslexia: Phonological and Processing Deficit in Developmental Dyslexia*. Bern: Peter Lang.

Vender, M., Delfitto, D., & Melloni, C. (2018). Clitic production and bilingualism: When exposure matters. *Languages, 3*, 1–17. https://doi.org/10.3390/languages3030022

Vender, M., Delfitto, D., & Melloni, C. (2020). How do bilingual dyslexic and typically developing children perform in nonword repetition? Evidence from a study on Italian L2 children. *Bilingualism: Language and Cognition, 23*(4), 884–896. https://doi.org/10.1017/S1366728919000828

Vender, M., Garraffa, M., Sorace, G., & Guasti, M. (2016). How early L2 children perform on Italian clinical markers of SLI: A study of clitic production and nonword repetition. *Clinical Linguistics and Phonology, 30*, 150–169. https://doi.org/10.3109/02699206.2015.1120346

Vender, M., & Guasti, M. (2020). L'apprendimento della letto-scrittura nei bambini con Italiano L2. In E. Bidese., J. Casalicchio., & M. Moroni (eds.), *Linguistics: Views from the Alps: Language Theory, Didactics and Society* (pp. 241–267). Peter Lang.

Vender, M., Hu, S., Mantione, F., Delfitto, D., & Melloni, C. (2018b). The production of clitic pronouns: A study on bilingual and monolingual dyslexic children. *Frontiers in Psychology*, 9, 2301. https://doi.org/10.3389/fpsyg.2018.02301

Vender, M., Hu, S., Mantione, F., Savazzi, S., Delfitto, D., & Melloni, C. (2018a). Bilingualism, dyslexia and morphological awareness: Evidence for an advantage of bilingualism in dyslexia. *Journal of Bilingual Education and Bilingualism*, 24(2), 1–18. https://doi.org/10.1080/13670050.2018.1450355

Vingerhoets, G., Van Borsel, J., Tesink, C., van den Noort, M., Deblaere, K., Seurinck, R., Vandemaele, P., & Achten, E. (2003). Multilingualism: An fMRI study. *NeuroImage*, 20(4), 2181–2196. https://doi.org/10.1016/j.neuroimage.2003.07.029

Voits, T., Robson, H., Rothman, J., & Pliatsikas, C. (2022). The effects of bilingualism on hippocampal volume in ageing bilinguals. *Brain Structure and Function*, 227, 979–994.

Volterra, V. (2014). Chi ha paura della lingua dei segni? *Psicologia Clinica dello Sviluppo*, 3, 425–477.

Volterra, V., & Taeschner, T. (1978). The acquisition and development of language by bilingual children. *Journal of Child Language*, 5(2), 311–326. https://doi.org/10.1017/S0305000900007492

Voss, M. W., Heo, S., Prakash, R. S., Erickson, K. I., Alves, H., Chaddock, L., Szabo, A., Mailey, E., Wójcicki, T., White, S., Gothe, N., McAuley, E., Sutton, B., & Kramer, A. F. (2013). The influence of aerobic fitness on cerebral white matter integrity and cognitive function in older adults: Results of a one-year exercise intervention. *Human Brain mapping*, 34(11), 2972–2985. https://doi.org/10.1002/hbm.22119

Voss, M.W., Nagamatsu, L.S., Liu-Ambrose, T., & Kramer, A.F. (2011). Exercise, brain, and cognition across the life span. *Journal of Applied Physiology*, 111(5), 1505–1513.

Wartenburger, I., Heekeren, H. R., Abutalebi, J., Cappa, S. F., Villringer, A., & Perani, D. (2003). Early setting of grammatical processing in the bilingual brain. *Neuron*, 37(1), 159–170. https://doi.org/10.1016/s0896-6273(02)01150-9

Weikum, W. M., Vouloumanos, A., Navarra, J., Soto-Faraco, S., Sebastián-Gallés, N., & Werker, J. F. (2007). Visual language discrimination in infancy. *Science*, *316*(5828), 1159. https://doi.org/10.1126/science.1137686

Werker, J., & Tees, R. (2005). Speech perception as a window for understanding plasticity and commitment in language systems of the brain. *Developmental Psychobiology*, *46*, 233–251. http://dx.doi.org/10.1002/dev.20060

Wingfield, A., & Tun, P. (2007). Cognitive supports and cognitive constraints on comprehension of spoken language. *Journal of the American Academy of Audiology*, *18*(7), 548–558. http://dx.doi.org/10.3766/jaaa.18.7.3

Winkler, I., Kujala, T., Tiitinen, H., Sivonen, P., Alku, P., Lehtokoski, A., Cziger, I., Csépe, V., Ilmoniemi, R. J., & Näätänen, R. (1999). Brain responses reveal the learning of foreign language phonemes. *Psychophysiology*, *36*(5), 638–642. https://doi:10.1111/1469-8986.3650638

Yip, V., & Matthews, S. (2007). *The Bilingual Child: Early Development and Language Contact (Cambridge Approaches to Language Contact)*. Cambridge: Cambridge University Press.

Zelazo, P. (2006). The dimensional change card sort (DCCS): A method of assessing executive function in children. *Nature Protocols*, *1*(1), 297–301. https://doi.org/10.1038/nprot.2006.46

INDEX